"Tremendous! Today we live in what are unquestionably interesting times, where success ultimately depends on our ability to devote all of our intelligence, creativity, and energy to the present moment. Maria Gonzalez's inspiring new book provides us with a holistic guide to leadership. Its nine specific ways of being are brilliant in their simplicity and will guide us on the road to achieving our personal and professional dreams."

—Peter R. Schaefer, President and CEO, Hannover Life Reassurance Company of America

"This is a down-to-earth and realistic guide to becoming a great leader and a better, happier human being. It is the most readable and motivating book on leadership that I have read in a very long time. It demystifies both mindfulness and leadership by giving easy-to-follow examples and exercises. Whether you are a CEO or just starting your career, this book will give you some simple ways to start to improve your performance today."

—Janet Martin, President, Janet C. Martin Management (and former EVP, Retail Banking CIBC)

"*Mindful Leadership* is a serious guide to helping you reset and reshape your crackdown rhythms in a manner that allows for a richer and more meaningful life—personally and professionally! It provides great tips and techniques to help make more sense out of one's 'fuzzy set' and encourages you to accept, adopt, and adapt to current conditions. In summary, *Mindful Leadership* positions you to lead and live with greater confidence and increased clarity."

—Mike Pado, CEO, Aurigen USA Holdings Inc.

"I love this book. It is very easy to read and understand, and a great guide to achieve clarity and purpose in what is truly important to you and your business. Whether you prefer to learn step-by-step or by allowing information to wash over you, the techniques can't help but benefit anyone who wants to lead well. The insights and practical tools in *Mindful Leadership* are invaluable for anyone who wants to be a good leader in all aspects of their life—work and personal."

—Rob Quartly, Juno Award–Winning Filmmaker and Entrepreneur

Mindful
Leadership

Mindful Leadership

*The 9 Ways to
Self-Awareness,
Transforming Yourself,
and Inspiring Others*

Maria Gonzalez

JOSSEY-BASS
A Wiley Imprint
www.josseybass.com

Library and Archives Canada Cataloguing in Publication

Gonzalez, Maria, 1958–
  Mindful leadership: The 9 ways to self-awareness, transforming yourself,
and inspiring others / Maria Gonzalez.

Includes bibliographical references and index.
ISBN 978–1–118–12711–7

    1. Leadership—Psychological aspects. 2. Meditation.
I. Title.

HD57.7.G65 2012   658.4'092   C2011–907375–7

ISBN 978–1–118–12818–3 (ebk); 978–1–118–12819–0 (ebk);
978–1–118–12820–6 (ebk)

Production Credits
Interior design: Pat Loi
Cover design: Adrian So
Cover photo credits: Thinkstock/Hemera
Production Editor: Lindsay Humphreys
Typesetter: Thomson Digital

John Wiley & Sons Canada, Ltd.
6045 Freemont Blvd.
Mississauga, Ontario
L5R 4J3

Printed in the United States of America

HB Printing   10 9 8

This book is dedicated to my family:
Gaetano, Alvarina, and Peanut;
and my teachers:
Shinzen Young and Joshu Sasaki Roshi

Contents

Acknowledgments

It takes a great deal of inspiration and support to write a book, and I have been blessed to have both. I have had the good fortune of having numerous mindful leaders in my life who have each been an inspiration in their own way.

I would like to thank a number of people who supported the creation of this book. They include:

My husband, Gaetano Geretto, who is one of the most mindful leaders I have ever met. He is an inspiration to me. I am deeply grateful for his constant support, advice, encouragement, and meticulous proofreading. I am blessed to share my life with a bodhisattva. He is one of those rare people who exhibits deep grace regardless of circumstance and who inspires others to greatness. His insights about leadership have been invaluable. Without his unwavering support this book could not have been written.

My mother, Alvarina Gonzalez, who has exhibited more personal leadership throughout her life than anyone I have known. She is the first bodhisattva I ever knew. I am deeply grateful for her strength, encouragement, compassion, and support. This book would not have been possible without her.

Peanut has been my loyal and constant companion during the entire writing process and has taught me a great deal about wisdom, compassion, and pure love.

Joshu Sasaki Roshi, who has shown me ultimate potential. He sets the highest of standards, and I am deeply grateful for his teaching; it has been invaluable. In his 105th year of life he exemplifies mindful leadership in every breath.

My teacher, Shinzen Young, for his skillful coaching, support, and infinite patience. He is a gifted teacher and mindful leader who makes the incomprehensible comprehensible and simple, but, of course, not too simple. His innovative mindfulness techniques have made the 2,500-year-old science of the mind accessible to our contemporary culture. Several of Shinzen's teachings are contained and cited in Chapter 2 and some of his techniques are described in Chapter 3. You can visit his website at www.basicmindfulness.org and view him on YouTube on the Expansion and Contraction channel.

Diana Byron, for her flawless editing, support, and skillful eye. Every book requires a great editor, and she is unparalleled. This book could not have been published without her.

Peter Pacini has made possible the Mindful Leadership blog, newsletter, and audio recordings of guided meditations that accompany this book. His support has been invaluable. He is a pleasure to work with and has enthusiasm, compassion, and a can-do attitude like none other.

Susan Smith, for her research, presence of mind, compassion, and ongoing support.

Janet Martin, for her insights on leadership. She is a mindful leader in her own right.

It has been a pleasure and privilege to coach hundreds of business leaders and professionals, as well as those who have participated regularly in my classes, workshops, and retreats. Their dedication to living and working mindfully has been an inspiration for this book.

The entire team at Wiley. Particular thanks go to Karen Milner, executive editor, for her enthusiasm, flexibility, and encouragement throughout the process and for her support for this project; she immediately understood the value in the message. And to Jennifer Smith, vice president and publisher, for her foresight in believing in this project. Once again, she understood that these times require out-of-the-mainstream thinking applied to the mainstream in order to help us move forward, and she knew that it would benefit readers to hear the message.

Part 1

Mindfulness

Chapter 1

Overview

Since the fall of 2008 we have seen trillions of dollars disappear from the global economy, causing a substantial restructuring. Indeed, few economies, organizations, or institutions in the world have been spared. Never in recent history have we had so much and lost so much. This is resulting in new realities for, and new expectations from, the global population. Through this economic crisis and its aftermath, many people have experienced disappointment in their leaders, whether they are business leaders, government leaders, celebrities, or top athletes.

During difficult times, anyone in a leadership position is scrutinized more closely. And it seems as if the demands of this new world order are beyond the experience of many who occupy leadership positions. The new reality requires all leaders to have an unprecedented presence of mind as a starting point from which to lead. Success hinges on the ability to effectively work with constant change and a state of impermanence. Ultimately, it will be mindful leadership that will help you navigate through these demanding times and unfamiliar waters.

> The biggest difference that mindfulness has made for me is that I now operate from a place of equanimity. I no longer live on a roller coaster. In the past, I was very much attached to outcomes, whether it was winning the deal, increasing sales, or hiring the very best staff. When I won it felt great, and when I didn't it was tough. Now I do the best I can, as I did in the past, but I let the chips fall where they may. Ironically, things work out better. Not trying to control every outcome allows me to learn from each situation. Mindfulness has given me far better balance. That's how I see equanimity, as balance. And because I don't ride the roller coaster anymore, I can sustain performance and feel more resilient. I'm a better leader and run a better business.
>
> —Financial services firm CEO

The strict definition of a leader as the person who heads up an organization or a nation is no longer a useful definition. A leader is anyone who is in a position to influence another person. This may be a CEO, the leader of a nation, the head of a government agency or department, the head of a professional services firm, a department head in a university or a hospital, a call center manager, a sports coach, an athlete, or any celebrity who has the potential to influence others. Indeed, every one of us is a leader. Leadership is much less a role than an activity.

To be an effective leader of others, you must first start with self-leadership. One of the keys to self-leadership is being mindful. Mindfulness is simply noticing the way things are.

By being mindful you can transform your life, your organization, and even your community. The first step is to transform yourself.

> One of the biggest lessons for me was what actually happens when you are present, right here right now. I used to delude myself that I could do several things at the same time. I would always multitask. I would be in a meeting and I would be on my BlackBerry answering e-mails and preparing for the next meeting. I thought that I was being efficient. But I was really being impatient. With mindfulness, however, I realized that I was missing fabulous opportunities to learn something about a client, the competition, or a business rival in any given meeting. By being present and mindfully listening, I learn a great deal that I would previously have missed. I hear what is actually being said and, potentially, what is being withheld. It's invaluable. Being present makes me more effective. An added bonus is that it also shortens my meetings. When I'm present, it takes less time to do everything, things don't get repeated, and we accomplish much more in less time.
>
> —Manufacturing company COO

My experience coaching and teaching mindfulness to hundreds of business leaders and professionals is that the following ways of being are key determinants of professional and personal success. Mindful leaders behave coherently and consistently, and exhibit nine specific ways of being:

1. They are *present*. This means that they are in the moment. They aim to be right here right now, rather than thinking about the past or worrying about the future.

2. They are *aware*. They know exactly what is arising within them at any given moment. This means they won't be blindsided by their emotions or negative patterns.

3. They are *calm*. Being calm allows them to keep their wits about them and increases the likelihood that those around them won't panic. Regardless of circumstances, they are able to face any situation without losing control.

4. They are *focused*. When leaders are focused, they deliberately channel resources to accomplish priorities, rather than being scattered. They are able to concentrate on whatever they deem important in any given moment.

5. They are *clear*. Being clear is critical in order to make the best possible decisions. Mindful leaders understand what motivates them and why they are drawn to take certain action. They know what is important.

6. They are *equanimous*. Equanimity is the ability to accept "what is" without resistance. To be equanimous is to truly have inner peace, because you do not waste time fighting what you can't change and you do not fight yourself. There is coherence in your being. You do not need for everything to be ideal in order to be content or even happy.

7. They are *positive*. This means that they are positive forces in their lives, organizations, families, and communities. And in so doing, they become an inspiration to those around them. They understand that the role of a leader is to be of service.

8. They are *compassionate*. Leaders who are compassionate have deep caring without attachment. They do their best each and every moment of the day, under the circumstances. They understand the importance and value of self-compassion, because they know that without taking care of themselves, their ability to serve and to perform at a high level is not sustainable.

9. They are *impeccable*. Mindful leaders are impeccable in their words and deeds. (But being impeccable should never be confused with being perfect.) They have integrity, are honest and courageous. They accept responsibility for their actions and do not blame others for honest mistakes.

There are countless resources advocating different leadership styles, but those styles tend to be faddish. Leaders searching for solutions often adopt whatever style is currently in vogue; however, then they cease to be authentic. This inevitably leads to inconsistent decisions, confusion, and dissatisfied stakeholders who recognize that the leader is hiding behind a facade. On the other hand, mindfulness can help leaders to remain focused on what really matters to them and to their companies and stakeholders. This allows them to lead from a place of authenticity.

Mindful leadership entails being aware of one's internal compass. It enables a leader to respond to a situation as it arises, to respond to the reality of constant change from a place of deep calm and focus, and to have the presence of mind to face the reality of any situation. A mindful leader is clear in his or her communication, and those he or she leads know that decisions are made from a place of awareness, integrity, and courage. A mindful leader inspires others to greatness, to achieve beyond their expectations.

> Mindfulness has changed my leadership so that I am not so focused on the short term. In the past, I might have done what was most expedient, and sometimes that meant exercising power inappropriately by bullying someone or berating them publicly to get the results I wanted. It may have worked in the short term, but in the long term it created resentment. It got in the way of long-term sustainable relationships. Now my main interest is to draw out the best in people. Sometimes it takes a bit more time, but you generate much more goodwill and trust, and people perform better and feel better about working on the team. In the long run, everyone wins.
>
> —Technology company executive

Mindfulness meditation and mindfulness principles provide leaders with a way to incorporate mindfulness into every aspect of their lives, allowing them to reduce stress, to maintain awareness and focus, and to optimize their effectiveness and decision making, both personally and professionally.

People sometimes worry that meditation is too New Agey for them or that it has religious connotations. Not so with Mindfulness meditation. It is simple, secular, and completely accessible to the mainstream. It's a tool that you can use anytime, anywhere—no chanting or patchouli required. This book will help you learn how to use mindfulness to transform your life and your business.

Phil Jackson, the coach of the Los Angeles Lakers—and noted as the coach with the greatest number of NBA Championship titles—is well known for his meditation practice. Many business leaders practice meditation as a way to become more effective, including Robert Shapiro, former Monsanto chief executive; William George, supervisory board member of the Goldman Sachs Group; William Ford, chairman of the Ford Motor Company; Steve Jobs, the late cofounder of Apple; and Robert Stiller, chairman of Green Mountain Coffee Roasters. Google began offering its staff Mindfulness meditation classes in 2007. Fred Shoemaker, the highly regarded golf coach, successfully applies mindfulness principles to coaching pros and new players alike. Since 1991, I have been applying Mindfulness meditation to every aspect of my business, including developing strategy, creating joint ventures and mergers and acquisitions, and negotiating deals around the world.

Mindfulness is not a technique, it's a skill—one that you can learn. Mindfulness meditation helps to train your mind to become more aware and to stay in the present moment.

Benefits of Mindfulness meditation in the worlds of business and leadership include:

- Greater focus and concentration
- Improved time management
- Improved judgment and decision making
- An enhanced ability to anticipate and serve stakeholder needs
- Increased ability to deal with conflict
- Enhanced team effectiveness
- Greater innovation and inspiration
- Greater productivity
- Increased ability to deal effectively with stress

Mindfulness begins with the simple act of being present in any given moment. Here are some easy ways to incorporate it into your life:

- When dealing with a challenging investment analyst meeting, use mindfulness in action to really listen. Rather than refuting or defending what is being said, simply become present and listen. This reduces the potential defensiveness that can easily occur when we feel criticized. You can then formulate a more coherent and less defensive response, so you and your organization will be in greater control.

- When making a presentation, become aware of the cues in the audience so you can determine if you need to clarify your message on the spot. Allow information to move freely from you to the audience and back again as a feedback loop even without them speaking to you.

- Before you get out of bed each morning, take the time to become aware of your body and your surroundings. Be present in that moment and allow yourself to be still; this is how inspiration arises. It will also make you feel more in control of your day.

- When the phone rings, use it as a cue to really listen. Take a deep breath before answering it, and focus on what the caller is saying. Do not multitask and answer e-mail at the same time; you will end up having to redo the e-mails or ask callers to repeat themselves.

- While in a meeting, you may find yourself drifting off. Try to really concentrate on the voice of the speaker; become aware of both the voice and the tone. You will gain insight into what the speaker is saying and not saying, and you will also be more alert and less stressed.

Mindful Leadership is a guide for businesspeople, leaders in the public service, professionals, anyone in a position to influence others, and those who aspire to be in a formal leadership position. Essentially, it will help anyone looking for a better way to lead. To be optimally effective, leaders must be clear about who and what they are and how they can best be of service to those they lead. Leaders cannot do it all on their own. They need to capture the imaginations and gain the support of those around them in order to be truly successful.

This includes clearly communicating an organization's vision, strategic direction, and goals, as well as how it will serve and compete in the marketplace. After all, without clarity, there is only confusion. This book will guide you to achieve clarity about what is truly important to you and to your business. *Mindful Leadership* will show you how to avoid loss of clarity by reducing the stresses in your life and effectively managing whatever ones remain so that you can be optimally effective regardless of circumstances. You'll also learn how to become resilient and to sustain high performance over the long term.

My goal is to help you experience greater fulfillment and success. Mindfulness is a learnable skill that can be used by anyone who wishes to become a more effective leader. The strategies in this book will help you to increase mindfulness in every aspect of your life, both professional and personal. By becoming calm and focused, being clear and applying equanimity, you'll be able to successfully lead your organization and your team—competing effectively today and successfully positioning yourself and your organization for tomorrow.

Chapter 2

An Introduction to Mindfulness Meditation

Mindfulness is simply noticing the way things are. It's not a technique, it's a skill—the skill of being aware without grasping or denying. Both grasping and denying are created states; they don't occur naturally. Therefore, mindfulness is the skill of being natural. It enables you to be aware of exactly who and what you are.

Mindfulness is rooted in a 2,500-year-old science of the mind called vipassana. Translated, "vipassana" means insight meditation or Mindfulness meditation. Although the ancient science of meditation began in Buddhism, it can be taught and practiced without religious beliefs and is applicable to the challenges of modern-day life, and to leadership in particular. Indeed, it's increasingly gaining popularity today, with such high-profile people as Oprah Winfrey, Phil Jackson, Richard Gere, Sting, Sheryl Crow, Leonard Cohen, k.d. lang, Shania Twain, Paul McCartney, Ringo Starr, Tina Turner, Goldie Hawn, Al Gore, William Ford (of the Ford Motor Company), and the late Steve Jobs, among many others, all praising the benefits of a meditation practice.

Mindfulness meditation trains us to be attentive and conscious about what's happening in any given moment through the use of specific techniques. It's the method or technique of intentionally becoming natural—which sounds like an oxymoron—but it works. Mindfulness meditation trains the mind to be in the present moment without distractions, and to concentrate on whatever you choose, for as long as you choose.[1]

As you use Mindfulness meditation techniques to train your mind, you gain control of it. An untrained mind tends to be controlled by thoughts and feelings, and is subject to much greater outside influence. For example, the success of a competitor at your expense, difficult conversations, poor results in the financial markets, or the receipt of bills can all negatively impact an untrained mind much more than one that is trained to allow distractions to arise without reacting to them and that can see them for what they are. Essentially, an untrained mind can become a runaway train. It can take away your inner peace, happiness, and state of well-being, negatively impacting your judgment and ability to make sound decisions.

Mindfulness meditation uses specific techniques and exercises that help you deepen your ability to concentrate (I discuss these techniques in Chapter 3). When you exercise your body with the proper techniques, you become stronger, more flexible, and have greater endurance. Likewise, the more you exercise your brain by meditating using the proper techniques, the more deeply you'll be able to concentrate and the greater clarity you'll achieve—about yourself, your business, and the world around you. In addition, you'll begin to experience *equanimity*, which refers to the ability to accept "what is arising within you" without resistance and to accept what you can't change. With training, you'll experience equanimity about the financial markets or about unexpected or uncontrollable challenges on key company projects. You'll continue to change what you can about your business so that it's more in line with your company's vision, strategy, and risk appetite, and you'll accept what you can't change, such as interest rates, foreign exchange rates, and analyst reports.

Basically, with equanimity you become increasingly aware of what can and cannot be changed, and you are better able to take advantage of opportunities previously unseen. When you don't sweat the small stuff or that which you cannot change, you have renewed energy to impact the things you *can* change.

The broad application of this ancient science of the mind requires techniques that are accessible in our contemporary culture. My main teacher, Shinzen Young, has made a significant contribution with his innovative mindfulness techniques. Like good science, the techniques are elegant and simple to teach. A number of his teachings are contained and cited in this chapter, and some of the techniques are described in Chapter 3.

Train Your Brain

Dr. Richard Davidson, a neuroscientist and experienced meditator, has been studying the results of meditation at the University of Wisconsin–Madison since 1992. A 2005 *Washington Post* article noted "The newest results from his studies take neuroplasticity a step further by showing that mental training through meditation . . . can in itself change the inner workings and circuitry of the brain. . . . Meditation not only changes the workings of the brain in the short term, but also quite possibly produces permanent changes."[2]

Dr. Davidson's research shows that meditation results in improvements in mental activities such as focus, memory, and learning, and leads to heightened awareness, as well as positive thoughts, emotions, and traits like optimism and resilience. He has concluded that in addition to these short-term benefits, meditation training and practice may produce permanent changes in the brain. And the really good news is that modern neuroscience shows that our minds are as elastic as our bodies and can be trained to improve at any age. Dr. Davidson says, "What we found is that the longtime practitioners [of meditation] showed brain activation on a scale we have never seen before. . . . Their mental practice is having an effect on the brain in the same way golf or tennis practice will enhance performance." This demonstrates, he says, that the brain is capable of being trained and physically modified in ways few people had imagined.[3]

Key Concepts

Throughout this book I use four concepts that are key in Mindfulness meditation: *equanimity, concentration, clarity*, and *purification*.

Equanimity

Equanimity refers to the ability to accept what is without resistance. After all, if something's already so, what's the benefit of resisting? Equanimity refers to accepting things you can't control in a given moment. And it refers to not denying or suppressing your thoughts and emotions. You can't control the financial markets or your company's market value, so being equanimous about these is a healthy strategy. Of course, this doesn't mean you must accept everything as is and not make changes. If you're unhappy with a situation and are in a position to change it, then do so. If you can make appropriate changes to your company's risk structure and maintain a calm perspective, then by all means do so. I'm not advocating a passive or indifferent attitude, but rather a gentle matter-of-factness with your sensory experience. Literally, "equanimity" means balance; in practical terms it means don't fight with yourself. It refers to an attitude of not interfering with the operation of the six senses (hearing, seeing, smelling, tasting, the thinking mind, and the feeling body) or sensory experience.[4] For example, if you are unhappy with a team member's performance and his or her improvement is unlikely, equanimity in this situation means accepting the emotions that this generates within you and making the necessary changes when appropriate.

Concentration

Concentration is the ability to keep your undivided attention on something you choose for as long as you choose. When you are mindful, you're able to allow distractions to remain in the background while you focus on the task at hand. A positive cycle arises whereby your ability to concentrate makes you feel calmer and, in turn, your calmness facilitates greater concentration. The more you're able to concentrate, the deeper your clarity becomes. Your increasing ability to focus and concentrate will make you more effective and efficient, freeing up time and allowing you to stay on plan and to see opportunities that previously may have been obscured. You'll be able to stay focused on what matters. For example, when you listen to a presentation, you'll be able to stay completely focused. This allows you to more easily see the points of integration among various businesses within your company, say, or previously unforeseen opportunities. Essentially, concentration enables you to listen more strategically.

Clarity

Clarity pertains to being clear and aware of what is going on, both internally and in the world at large. The greater your clarity, the better you're able to make decisions, because you understand what drives you. This includes times when you distract yourself because you're uncomfortable about something you've become aware of or realized. As a leader, clarity about your company's vision and mission and your own life's purpose will make it less likely that you'll become clouded by short-term financial results or any other external influences.

Purification

Purification refers to the clearing away of negative, habitual patterns. We all have sources of unhappiness within us; when you clear yours away, you can experience true freedom. As you observe what arises internally and do nothing to interfere, you experience purification. This results in dissolving the blockages to happiness—you reveal your intrinsic happiness, the nature of your consciousness, which is effortless joy.[5] Suddenly you'll start to experience true liberation, and this frees up a tremendous amount of energy. This can be particularly beneficial if you've previously developed an unhealthy relationship with power and money.

In Mindfulness meditation, extraordinary attention is paid to ordinary experience. This attention, when applied with equanimity, produces insight and purification. The insight attained is a deep understanding about profound universal issues, such as how it is that pain turns into suffering, how it is that pleasure becomes satisfaction or neediness, and how it is that the sense of self arises.[6] When you observe what's happening, particularly internally, and don't interfere, you experience purification, which dissolves blockages to happiness. It takes a lot of energy to try to control everything and ensure that things are exactly "right." When you stop doing this, you'll start to experience liberation and to free up energy. You'll have a sense of freedom and happiness that isn't dependent on conditions or circumstances. When you apply equanimity, you're more powerful because your actions come from a place of awareness and nonattachment— hence, decisions are made based on fact rather than emotion.

During the financial meltdown in the fall of 2008, those who were trained in mindfulness and were able to apply equanimity to their situations were less likely to make rash decisions about their business strategies or their personal portfolios; they were able to consider all of the implications before making decisions and taking action. They were able to listen to the facts, rather than falling prey to their fears of what might be looming in the future. Recognizing that these markets were unpredictable, they focused on what they could control rather than on what they couldn't. Despite experiencing anxiety, they allowed it to fully arise in them without resistance and without catastrophizing about what might be. Therefore, they were able to control their minds and didn't suffer as they would have if they'd allowed their thoughts to run wild.

When it came to making business decisions, they were able to incorporate a longer-term perspective and maintain a macroview, rather than reacting to what was happening in the short term. In effect, they responded to the circumstances rather than reacting, and were able to continue to be effective leaders.

The Price of Stress

Stress is so commonplace now it just seems like a way of life. Competition is increasingly fierce and global. The expectations of a 24/7 connectedness are unsustainable and drain energy. The fear of losing ground keeps us trying to do the impossible. In an effort to stay afloat, we increase our multitasking, which causes even greater stress and makes us less competent. The research on multitasking has been consistent for decades, but we persist in the face of scientific evidence that tells us that it is not possible to multitask effectively. In fact, recent research from Stanford University is startling. Researchers found that most persistent multitaskers perform badly on a variety of tasks. They don't focus as well as non-multitaskers. They are more distractible. They're weaker at shifting from one task to another and at organizing information. The multitaskers could not help thinking about the task they weren't doing. They are, in fact, worse at multitasking than people who don't ordinarily multitask.[7]

All of this stress comes at a price. Over time, it affects our ability to make decisions, our judgment, our relationships, and our health. To maintain well-being, it's important to develop and cultivate the "relaxation response" (a term coined at Harvard Medical School in the 1970s by Dr. Herbert Benson).[8] Essentially, the relaxation response is the ability to create calm at will. With practice, mindfulness will enable you to do just that.

Humans are equipped with a basic fight-or-flight instinct that dates back to cave-dwelling times. In those days it was very beneficial—your brain didn't wait around to find out if the threatening noise behind you came from a mammoth or saber-toothed cat; sensing danger, it told you to run. This was essential for the preservation of the species. In modern times, however, it's rarely an appropriate response. But because the human brain is still wired the same way, the fight-or-flight instinct can still be raised. If you're sitting in a meeting and you sense something going wrong, it's probably inappropriate to run—but, unfortunately, the response is still activated. Unless you're able to relax yourself and work through the adrenaline, it stays in your system as stress and negatively affects you, both physically and emotionally. The bottom line is that when you're stressed, you're driven by fear or worry, your system isn't at ease, and your well-being is compromised.

With meditation practice you'll be able to create a gap between stimulus and response (a phrase coined by Viktor Frankl) and, with further practice, to widen that gap.[9] The more you practice mindfulness, the wider that gap can become, and this makes it easier to create and maintain perspective when you're making decisions. This helps to keep stress at bay, and rather than being driven by emotion and behaving irrationally and impulsively, you'll be able to calmly and clearly assess a situation and make better decisions. At the same time, you'll lessen the physiological stress on yourself.

The following stress-related statistics are quite clear, and a sad reality of our time. And consider that many of these were compiled before the 2008 market collapse and economic recession. In fact, these statistics were compiled in a time of unprecedented prosperity. Just imagine how much worse they'll be going forward:

- U.S. companies lose an estimated $200 billion annually in absenteeism, subpar performance, tardiness, and workers' compensation claims related to stress.[10] In smaller economies like Australia, the results are equally significant, with work stress costing $15 billion per year.[11]

- Stress-related ailments account for more than 60 percent of visits made to doctors.[12]

Benefits of Mindfulness Meditation

Interesting things happen when you practice the techniques of Mindfulness meditation. The first thing you'll experience is a greater sense of calm. You'll feel more relaxed. Over time, situations that once caused stress don't seem worth worrying about. Life seems more pleasant and fulfilling. You'll be better able to savor positive experiences and deal with difficult or painful ones. You'll have more confidence in your ability to handle life's adversities, such as illness, economic crisis, or professional hardship. While the difficulty will still exist, being equanimous makes it bearable. When you're equanimous, you accept what is and make better decisions because you're able to keep your wits about you. As well, mindfulness training dramatically increases your general concentration ability. This is critical because concentration power is the single most universally applicable and most deeply empowering skill that a human being can cultivate.

Much research has been done on the physiological effects of reducing stress and Mindfulness meditation's role in this. Mindfulness meditation provides a host of benefits in people's lives, both personally and professionally. The following benefits are consistently reported by the people I coach and the organizations I work with, including:

Personal/Health Benefits

- A brain rewired for greater focus and happiness
- Improved immune system
- Lowered blood pressure
- A healthier heart
- A reduction in chronic pain and a greater ability to manage it
- Decreased anxiety and better handling of stress
- Improved memory
- Improved ability to learn
- Regulated emotions
- Improved cognitive processing

Organizational/Professional Benefits

- Increased personal resilience and the ability to sustain performance
- Better judgment and decision making
- Improved concentration on the task at hand and an enhanced ability to stay focused, making one more effective
- An ability to prioritize
- Enhanced capacity to work on multiple projects because of an enhanced ability to focus on a single task in a given

moment, thereby becoming much more effective and efficient

- Improved time management
- Improved ability to problem solve by seeing situations with greater clarity
- An ability to more effectively coach or mentor staff
- Better handling of stressful situations and working more effectively under pressure
- Increased ability to listen to others and utilize valid feedback
- An ability to anticipate and serve client needs
- Creativity

When teams are trained jointly, they report:

- Improved team effectiveness, including more effective and efficient meetings of significantly shorter duration
- Improvement in team performance and fewer mis-understandings
- The ability to determine what underlies most conflicts and to arrive at a mutually beneficial conclusion
- Individuals and teams with greater innovation and inspiration
- Greater collaboration and cooperation, and joint prob-lem solving

- Enhanced communication within and across teams
- An enhanced ability to anticipate and serve client needs
- Greater compassion and empathy
- Overall greater productivity at all levels of the organization

In Summary

Overall, individuals who practice Mindfulness meditation report greater satisfaction with their lives and greater personal happiness. They describe an improved ability to connect with colleagues, family, and friends. They report less stress and a significantly improved ability to sleep. A common theme is their experience of a vastly improved quality of life.

You too can experience these benefits, but success requires two conditions. The first is *motivation*: you need to have an interest and desire to do this training of the mind, aimed at helping yourself. The other is *practice*: in order to experience benefits, you need to practice the proper techniques on, ideally, a daily basis. It's possible to experience benefit with as little as 10 to 15 minutes per day. Naturally, a daily investment of 20 to 30 minutes will bring about greater benefit, but the key is consistency and momentum. Better to practice for 10 minutes every day than 30 minutes twice per week.

One of the greatest immediate benefits of practicing mindfulness is the ability to gain control of your mind and thereby your life. This ability is imperative for personal and professional success. The beauty is that your baseline concentration, clarity, and equanimity increase permanently with continued practice.[13] As with physical exercise, the benefits that are derived from mindfulness practice aren't experienced only during the actual practice but throughout the entire day. In fact, you'll often become aware of how much your life has changed when an experience that previously would have seemed devastating is experienced as merely inconvenient or unfortunate, and manageable. A market crash or the loss of a major account can be experienced as disruptive and unfortunate, rather than devastating. In fact, with equanimity you can immediately go about making the changes that will be most advantageous to the situation.

The key message is simple: You can use the power of your mind to regain control of your mind. This enables you to create optimal effectiveness in your personal and professional lives. Mindfulness meditation becomes beneficial to your mental and physical health, to your happiness, to the prosperity of your organization, and, indeed, to society as a whole. Essentially, Mindfulness meditation has the potential to transform lives.

Still unsure about how something so seemingly simple can be so powerful? Read on to learn about some amazing findings.

The Research

Below is but a small sampling of the abundant scientific research that has been conducted on the effectiveness of meditation and the conclusions drawn by the scientific community:

- Men with coronary artery disease were able to improve their heart rate, blood pressure, and work performance by meditating 20 minutes twice daily for six to eight months.[14]

- Hospital admissions for cardiovascular disease were dramatically reduced among long-term meditators. Cardiologist Dr. John Zamarra from Southern California states, "There is more research on the benefits of meditation than any other medical procedure to improve health. It has been found that hospital admissions for cardiovascular disease were reduced by an astounding 87 percent among long-term meditators. The research was well controlled; these patients still had routine medical exams and physicals, so there was no confounding reason that they might have been merely avoiding medical care. If there was a cardiovascular drug that even approached 87 percent effectiveness, it would be considered a miracle drug."[15]

- A recent major study, the Shamatha Project, suggests that meditation can protect our chromosomes from degeneration. This potentially has stunning implications: that meditation might help delay the process of aging. This is the first study to suggest that meditation plays a role in cellular aging.[16]

- The most recent research on pain confirms that meditation enables people to better handle pain. In addition, the research found that meditation actually changes the nature of the pain before it is perceived, in effect reducing a person's sensitivity to pain by reducing the actual sensation.[17]

- Research has found Mindfulness meditation to be very effective in both the prevention of depression and in its treatment. Researchers have found a 44 percent reduction in the risk of relapse in those with a history of two or more depressions, a group that is typically challenging to treat.[18]

- In Australia, a country where 40 percent of the population experiences significant stress, a recent study found that workers who meditated became significantly less stressed and depressed.[19]

- According to the Center for Creative Leadership, the average worker is interrupted every 11 minutes. Even more interesting is that it then takes him or her about 25 minutes to get back to the original task.[20] Clearly, the issue of lost productivity is huge. No wonder we can end our day feeling like we've been very busy yet have not accomplished a great deal. With mindfulness training, no matter how often you're interrupted, it takes only seconds to return to your original task. This means that individuals who have a trained mind are able to accomplish a great deal in short periods, without being frustrated at having been interrupted. As well, tasks don't need to be done more than once, making such people more efficient and able to accomplish much more in a shorter time.

- Researchers have found that mindfulness can reprogram the brain to be more rational and less emotional. When faced with a decision, meditators showed increased activity in the posterior insula of the brain, which has been linked to rational decision making. This allowed them to make decisions based more on facts than emotion.[21] This is good news, since other research has found that reasoning is actually suffused with emotion. Not only are the two inseparable, but our positive and negative feelings about people, things, and ideas arise much more rapidly than our conscious thoughts, in a matter of milliseconds. We push threatening information away and hold friendly information close. We apply fight-or-flight reflexes not only to predators but to data itself.[22]

- Meditation appears to alter the brain's biochemistry: "For decades, researchers at the National Institutes of Health, the University of Massachusetts, and the Mind/Body Medical Institute at Harvard University have sought to document how meditation enhances the qualities companies need in their human capital: sharpened intuition, steely concentration, and plummeting stress levels. What's different today is groundbreaking research showing that when people meditate, they alter the biochemistry of their brains. The evolution of powerful mind-monitoring technologies such as MRIs and EEGs has also enabled scientists to scan the brains of meditators on a microscopic scale, revealing fascinating insights about the plasticity of the mind and meditation's ability to sculpt it."[23]

- "One of the strongest findings in neuroplasticity, the science of how the brain changes its structure and function in response to input, is that *attention* is almost magical in its ability to physically alter the brain and enlarge functional circuits. . . . The research suggests that cognitive training benefits only the task used in training and does not generalize to other tasks. However, meditation has been found to increase the thickness of regions of the brain that control attention and process sensory signals from the outside world."[24] For example, if you do a lot of crossword puzzles, you can improve your ability to do them. But this crossword puzzle skill does not transfer to other tasks. On the other hand, attention skills are fully transferable to all other things you do, and mindfulness and mindfulness training are about paying attention.

- Studies show that mind wandering is very common. People spend up to 50 percent of their time not thinking about the task at hand, even when they have been explicitly asked to pay attention. Studies show that we find it difficult to stay focused for more than a few minutes on even the easiest tasks, despite the fact that we make mistakes whenever we drift away.[25] Mindfulness training helps reduce mind wandering; with even greater experience, the mind hardly wanders at all, making you much more effective and efficient.

- A recent study at Harvard Medical School suggests that meditation may modulate those brain waves known as alpha rhythms, which help regulate the transmission of sensory input from the surrounding environment. Imagine you are reading something in a noisy environment and you want to focus on what you are reading. You might use your alpha rhythms, like a volume knob, to turn down the volume on neurons that represent sound from the outside world. We all do this to some extent, but meditators become very skilled at it.[26] If you consider many open-space work environments, you can see why this is a valuable skill that can significantly contribute to greater productivity.

- Dr. Jon Kabat-Zinn is Professor of Medicine Emeritus and founding director of the Stress Reduction Clinic and the Center for Mindfulness in Medicine, Health Care, and Society at the University of Massachusetts Medical School. He has done extensive research on the health benefits of Mindfulness meditation, and he and Dr. Richard Davidson "collaborated on a recent study of workers in a high-tech company who took a two-month training program in meditation. It showed significant changes in brain activity, declines in anxiety, and beneficial changes in immune function."[27]

- In two companies that introduced meditation, managers and employees who regularly practiced meditation reported significant reductions in health problems such as headaches and backaches, improved quality of sleep, and a noteworthy reduction in the use of hard liquor and cigarettes, compared with personnel in the control groups.[28]

- Taking a few minutes in a day to slow down benefits individuals and organizations. According to Dr. Herbert

Benson, an American cardiologist and founder of the Mind/Body Medical Institute at Massachusetts General Hospital in Boston, who studied the relaxation response in the 1970s, "If businesses were clever, what they would do is simply put time aside [and have] a quiet room for people to carry out a meditative behavior of their choice."[29]

- The ability of employees to manage stress is a key factor in individual and organizational performance. As vice-chair and a founding member of the Global Business and Economic Roundtable on Addiction and Mental Health, I stated, "It has become clear to me that in order to create and sustain 'healthy organizations' it is imperative that the mental health of individuals at all levels of the organization be a priority. Our research on healthy organizations suggests that individuals experiencing undue stress are not able to perform optimally, thereby representing an opportunity cost in terms of organizational performance, significant corporate health care costs, and a significant cost to society at large."[30] In a *Globe and Mail* interview, I said, "As business leaders, one of our key interests is sustainable performance. There can be no sustainable performance without organizational health."[31]

You can clearly see that mindfulness works wonders on health and performance. When applied to leadership it has the potential to transform both your organization and the quality of your life.

Chapter 3

Mindfulness Techniques

You learned in Chapter 2 that it's possible for you to gain control of your mind by training it. Training your mind enables you to be a more effective leader, experience greater calm, have more peace of mind, make better decisions, discover what truly matters to you, and find fulfillment in your work and your life. In this chapter I describe generic mindfulness techniques that can be applied both to leadership and to life in general. In later chapters, I'll introduce you to techniques that can be particularly helpful with the various aspects of leadership, including developing greater self-awareness and an awareness of how you impact others.

To lead successfully, it's important to develop:

1. The ability to calm yourself in the face of stress or difficult decisions. This enables you to have a calming effect on those you lead.

2. The ability to understand what's going on within yourself and how you perceive your reality and the business reality. When you understand what drives you and how you think and feel about what arises, you'll have clear judgment, which makes decision making easier.

3. The ability to be in the present moment and clearly understand what you're hearing or reading, instead of being caught up in regretting or reliving the past or fearing and catastrophizing the future. This enables you to respond appropriately no matter what the circumstances.

4. The ability to imagine a life that is positive and fulfilling and to set in motion positive outcomes in your life and business. This enables you to create a vision and strategy for your life and your business based on your aspirations.

5. And finally, the ability to know that all things pass and that nothing is forever, whether it's good or bad. This applies equally to record-breaking quarters or disappointing returns, as well as to bull markets and market collapses.

Mindfulness can help you to develop all of the abilities listed above. The goal is, over time, to begin living mindfully throughout the day. To achieve this, you need to start meditating regularly, developing a daily (or almost daily) practice. This will allow you to experience greater calm and to develop focus or concentration, as well as to hone your intuition or gut feelings. The spillover benefits from adding a formal sitting meditating practice to your daily routine will occur naturally. But, in order to leverage the benefits of your formal practice and maximize their potential, you must also employ *mindfulness-in-action* strategies. These are specific strategies that you can use anytime—while leading a meeting, making a presentation, developing your business strategy, reading the stock ticker, buying a business, selling a business, walking the dog, driving, playing golf—you get the picture. Mindfulness is applicable to everything that occurs during your day, whether personal or professional. My coaching experience has shown me that clients who pay special attention to using mindfulness in their daily lives greatly accelerate their development of the skill of mindfulness. By applying these strategies consistently, such people are being proactive and, in time, they start to be mindful without conscious effort.

With this in mind, throughout the chapter I'll introduce you to techniques for both formal practice and strategies for mindfulness in action, which you can practice during your regular daily life. Don't panic and think you'll never be able to do this; I have never worked with anyone who was motivated to learn and who practiced regularly (even as little as 10 minutes per day) who couldn't do this and experience the benefits. When you first begin your practice, you may find the audio recordings of guided meditations featuring the various techniques described in this chapter at www.argonautaconsulting.com particularly helpful, as well as my blog on mindful leadership at www.argonautaconsulting.com/blog.

I would like to clarify a popular misconception that meditation is about clearing or emptying the mind and that in fact, the objective is to have no thoughts. Nothing could be further from the truth. There will be times when many thoughts arise. At times they may appear incessant. Other times there may be fewer thoughts. That is just the way it is. The thoughts themselves are not a problem. It is the pushing away or repressing of thoughts that is the problem. Just let thoughts do what they wish to do, without getting caught up in them. You will notice that they appear, disappear, rise and fall whether you are a beginner or an experienced meditator. It is our relationship to the thoughts that makes all the difference. The experienced meditator merely lets thoughts rise and fall with equanimity.

Relaxation Techniques

You can do these relaxation techniques sitting in a chair or lying down. Try them in both positions to see which best helps you reach maximum relaxation.

The Breath

We often tell someone who's visibly stressed to "take a breath," and there are sound reasons for this. Typically, when we're stressed our breath becomes shallow or uneven, which creates a cycle that causes even greater stress. By taking a conscious breath, you can slow things down. Make it a slow, even breath. You might try breathing in for a count of three or four and out for a count of three or four. Doing this for five minutes or so will relax you greatly. Try to pay attention only to the breath, and count as you are inhaling and exhaling. When you become distracted by your thoughts or they become critical ("This won't help one bit") or doubting ("I hope this helps, but what if it doesn't?"), very gently bring them back to the breath. At first you may need to bring yourself back to your breath dozens of times in, say, a five-minute period, but don't despair—distraction is perfectly normal.

Concentrating on your breathing is also a good strategy in daily life, one that can help calm you as you're about to start a meeting with analysts or about to have a difficult conversation. You may not need to practice conscious breathing for the full five minutes in these circumstances; just stopping to take one or two breaths may suffice to remind you to be mindful, to be in the present moment, and to not be hijacked by any runaway thoughts.

Think of the breath as your ally. It's an internal relaxation mechanism available to you 24 hours a day. You can consciously access it anytime you want to gain perspective or widen the gap between stimulus and response so that you can make better decisions. You can also use this technique as you lie in bed before going to sleep or when you wake up.

Body Relaxation

Another relaxation technique is to systematically relax your body. Begin with your feet. Relax them, letting go of any tension. Then move your way up to the lower leg, then the upper leg, continuing to work your way up to the torso, the shoulders and arms, the neck, and the head. As you're doing this, concentrate only on relaxing the body part you are focusing on and maintaining relaxation in the parts you have already focused on. As with the breath technique, if your mind wanders or your thoughts become critical, very gently bring it back into focus without judging yourself. When you have relaxed your whole body to the best of your ability, try to remain relaxed for a few more minutes. At this point your focus of concentration is the whole body and the enjoyment of being relaxed.

If you do this technique as a daily formal practice, you can do it in 10 to 30 minutes, depending on your available time. As you gain experience, you'll be able to relax your whole body in as little as five minutes, and eventually in seconds. This too is a technique you may benefit from doing just before bedtime for a deep rest or if you wake up at night and have difficulty falling back asleep. Rather than thinking about everything that you need to do in the morning—a sure way of not falling asleep—aim to relax your body.

Strategies for Mindfulness in Action

In daily life, you can use awareness as a strategy to calm your body at will. Train yourself to tune in to your body periodically during the day, and see whether you are holding tension anywhere. If you're like most people, you may have a particular part of the body that tightens under stress. Commonly this is the shoulders, the neck, the stomach, or the back, but it could be any part of the body. By tuning in periodically, you become more familiar with your body, as well as with situations that cause you stress.

For the first week, merely tune into the body throughout the day and pay attention to what you discover. Are you tense or relaxed? Is there a part (or parts) of the body that is often tense? Under what circumstances do you become tense? Simply become aware; change nothing. You may find that just by placing awareness on the tense area, you become more relaxed. Or you may realize how tense you actually are and not become relaxed at all. This is fine; all you're looking for during this first week is awareness.

After the first week, every time you tune into your body and find a tense area, purposefully relax it to the best of your ability. Notice that I said "to the best of your ability." You may find that at first your ability to relax systematically is very modest. Don't be concerned—it's not a problem. With persistence it will improve, so be prepared to amaze yourself. And remember too, every day is a different day, every moment a different moment: one day you may not be able to relax very much, while the next day you can relax completely. Be patient and don't let yourself become discouraged.

The following formal techniques described below of Internal Awareness, External Awareness, and Imagining Positive Outcomes were developed by Shinzen Young.

Three things matter when you perform these techniques:

1. *Concentration*, which means that you stay focused on what you are working with.

2. *Clarity*, which means that you know exactly what space you are noticing and what is arising.

3. *Equanimity*, which means that you accept whatever is arising internally with a gentle matter-of-factness.

Internal Awareness

Life is lived in the mind. Our perception is our reality. Sometimes we seem to be stuck in our heads, so to speak. We relive the past, thinking about how we could have better handled a situation. We worry about what might happen in the future: Will we perform well in our new role as leader? Have we made the right hiring decision? Was it the right acquisition? And on and on. For the most part, the worry and fear involves events that will never happen, and we all know that reliving the past won't change any of it, so why focus on either? Most of our mind space is consumed with the past or the future, but with a trained mind you can spend more time in the present moment, which is where life is lived. Remember that the mind is a trickster and not always reliable. You can't believe every thought or every feeling you have.

We all think in mental images and in mental talk that takes the form of us carrying on conversations in our own heads. We can also hear the voices of others in our heads, as when we "play back" a conversation that happened earlier in the day. This is our *thinking mind*. In terms of the thinking process, sometimes there's only *talk* or only *images*; other times the thinking mind may manifest as both images and talk.

We also experience *the feeling body*, which refers to physical sensations in the body that are associated with emotion. These may result from a mental image or mental talk and can be pleasant or unpleasant. In some instances, *feel* sensations in the body may arise independently of the thinking mind, as with our primitive reaction of, say, fear of the dark or fear of thunder. These sensations can occur anywhere in the body and may be very subtle or very strong and evident. Examples of the feeling body include tightness in your stomach when you're anxious, tightness in the throat when you can't say what you wish to say, the expanded sensation in your chest when you're joyful, or the curving up of your mouth when you smile.

Together, the thinking mind and the feeling body are a powerful combination. Marketers know this and use it to great benefit; they know that they can get consumers to act in their favor if they can motivate the feeling body, which is the greatest driver of behavior. Often marketing material shows an evocative image, to try to stimulate the feeling body; this is often done by appealing to one or more of the hindrances, explained in Chapter 4. Many thoughts, especially those that are emotionally charged or have a powerful grip on us, are experienced physically in the body. If you're not aware of their connection to the body, you can easily become hijacked by your thoughts and lose touch with the present moment and, often, with what matters. This can cause you to make poor decisions and unfair or inaccurate judgments, and to experience increased stress.

Here's an example of this powerful combination of the thinking mind and feeling body. Imagine replaying to yourself an interview for a leadership role you really want. It was a positive interview. In your mind's eye is an image of the interview or the setting where it took place. You remember the words the interviewer used to tell you that he looks forward to extending an offer. Along with the mental image and the mental talk, you have a pleasant sensation in your chest or perhaps even throughout your body.

Now imagine the opposite. Your present position is being eliminated, and you have just had an interview for another position you really want. The interviewer says she is very impressed with your qualifications but that you are not the right fit. You drive home, but you don't remember any of the drive. Instead, throughout the entire drive you saw the image of the office and the interviewer. Over and over again, you hear the interviewer say that you are not the right fit. Your stomach is in knots, your hands are clammy, and you are starting to get a tension headache. Now new images arise, images of losing your current position and being unemployed, of the conversation you will have with your family—who know how much you wanted this position—how unhappy you are, and how this situation is affecting the quality of your life. You imagine never finding a suitable position you will enjoy and losing your home because you may not be able to pay the mortgage. This brings about deeper sensations in your body. Now you experience nausea, your blood pressure rises, your heart rate accelerates, and your face flushes.

This is a clear example of the thinking mind and the feeling body reinforcing one another and escalating sensations, potentially to a state of panic. This is not an unusual reaction when you are in an unhappy situation professionally or when your position is being eliminated because of the sale of a business unit, say, or a downturn in the economy. You can well imagine how health becomes compromised and judgment becomes impaired in these moments. In this last example, you went from hearing a disappointing decision to catastrophizing that you would never find another job and would lose your home. Now, I'm not minimizing the significance of such a situation;

it's serious and unpleasant. But in this present moment, nothing has changed.

It's critical that you understand that the feeling body can drive behavior, and that this can seriously impair judgment. Imagine that you stay awake all night worrying, gripped by the fear of what will happen in the future. By morning you have decided to put your house up for sale before it's "too late." You ask your broker to price the house well below market so that it can be a quick sale. This may be the right thing to do; most likely it is not—impulsive decisions often are not wise. The fear in your body is simply so great that it drives you to act impulsively.

A trained mind will generally catch itself. If, keeping with the example, you are familiar with mindfulness techniques, you might have connected to your breath, slowed things down, and created some calm. You might have taken a few minutes to relax your body, which would have been quite tense. You would also have been aware of what your thinking mind and feeling body were experiencing, and not been hijacked by it. The technique of Internal Awareness enables you to divide and conquer what's arising so that you don't become overwhelmed. Over time, you'll realize that the feeling body and the thinking mind will arise and that you can untangle them, stopping them from escalating and spiraling out of control.

In fact, in time and with practice, some of these techniques would kick in automatically. You would be able to stay focused on the task at hand or the mindfulness technique you chose to follow. You would be clear about what was arising within yourself and able to apply equanimity to what you were experiencing. You wouldn't be fighting yourself. Your mind would be calm and sharp so that sound decisions would follow, and physiologically your system wouldn't be compromised. The relaxation response (introduced in Chapter 2) would kick in.

Pain and Suffering

A key point to consider in the discussion of Internal Awareness is the distinction between pain and suffering. *Pain* refers to the difficulties, physical and emotional, that arise in life. Pain is inevitable. This isn't a pessimistic view; it's just the reality of life. *Suffering*, on the other hand, is optional. Suffering occurs when you resist and aren't equanimous with whatever is arising in your sensory experience. As mentioned in Chapter 2, equanimity refers to an attitude of not interfering with the operation of the six senses (hearing, seeing, smelling, tasting, the thinking mind, and the feeling body). When you resist, not only do you suffer but you also perpetuate the suffering. The reality is that what you resist persists. Resisting what arises internally causes concentration, clarity, and equanimity to decrease, and as they decrease, suffering increases. According to Shinzen Young, "Pain is one thing and resistance to pain is something else, and when the two come together you have an experience of suffering . . . suffering is pain multiplied by resistance."[1]

In the second scenario of our example, the pain came from the fact that you were not being extended a job offer. The suffering is the catastrophizing and worrying about the future.

You were dealing with both the rejection and the extreme worry. You resisted admitting to yourself that you had not succeeded in the job competition and that you were overwhelmed by fear. You lost your focus and equanimity, and the moment lacked clarity. The more you resisted and interfered with what was arising within you, the more your suffering increased, and you were much more likely to make an impulsive decision in this state. However, if you had been trained in mindfulness, although you would still have experienced the pain of the rejection, you wouldn't have suffered. You would have allowed yourself to experience the pain fully instead of resisting it through worry or by trying to distract yourself from it with a drink or a piece of cake. By experiencing the pain fully you prevent suffering, because suffering = resistance × pain.[2] When there's no resistance, there's no suffering. You can see how quickly you can become overwhelmed by any situation if you're not mindful. Over time, this kind of stress can take a serious toll on your health and judgment and, as a consequence, on personal and professional effectiveness.

Formal Technique

You can practice the technique of Internal Awareness (I also refer to it as *feel*, *image*, and *talk*) either sitting up in formal meditation posture, which includes maintaining the back erect, or lying down.

Feel space: To start, place awareness on the parts of your body where you know you typically experience physical sensations that are associated with emotion. (This might include your stomach, where you hold tension, or your mouth, with which you smile or laugh with joy.) Feel can be pleasant or unpleasant, such as a spontaneous smile or a nervous stomach. You may find that at times you experience these sensations throughout your body, as when you're so filled with fear or joy that you experience it from head to toe.

Image space: Now, also place awareness on the mental screen where you typically perceive images when your eyes are closed. This is usually in front of or behind your closed eyes. You might think of this as the mind's eye.

Talk space: Finally, place awareness at your ears or around your head, wherever you typically hear the sound of your own voice or mental conversation.

Notice what arises in all three of these spaces. Pay attention to one thing at a time. You may find you're primarily aware of the feeling body or of one of the two components of the thinking mind (image or talk), or you may even experience all three at the same time. The key is to give attention to only one at a time, even if they all arise at once. Do this at a leisurely pace, and find your rhythm. For example, you may notice a tight stomach; stay focused on it for a few seconds. Then notice what else has come into your awareness—perhaps an image of your cottage. Stay focused on it for a few seconds. Then see what else has come into your awareness—maybe it's even your inner voice saying, "I feel really strange doing this."

It's entirely possible that in a given moment there is no activity in your feel, image, or talk spaces because the three spaces are *at rest*. At any given time any of the spaces can be active or restful. *All rest* occurs only if all three spaces are at rest at the same time; if they're not, draw your attention to an active space.

Practice this technique of Internal Awareness for at least 10 minutes at a time. With this technique, you pay extraordinary attention to ordinary experience. The more familiar you become with your thinking mind and feeling body, the less likely you are to be hijacked by stress or impulsiveness. The goal with this technique is not to experience total calm but to notice what is arising within you at any given moment. Just notice and don't interfere. Surrender to what arises. This is the equanimity I spoke about in Chapter 2.

Strategies for Mindfulness in Action

At first you may not think of checking in with yourself during the day, so to start, tune into the three spaces (feel, image, and talk) when you have any highly pleasant or unpleasant experiences. This will make you familiar with where you experience them in your body. If you're listening to a beautiful musical performance and enjoying it thoroughly, notice what's going on internally for you in these subjective spaces. Likewise, if you've just found out that a key player on your team has resigned, tune in to your body to see what's going on. Doing this will train you to be self-aware and prevent you from being hijacked. If you're unaware, you may sometimes carry with you throughout the day an unpleasant experience from the morning without realizing its cause; your mother might have called this "waking up on the wrong side of the bed." Train yourself to experience things fully as they happen so that you don't carry them around all day long. When you have a complete experience and apply equanimity moment by moment, life appears bearable and manageable, even under significant stress.

There are many opportunities to use this technique throughout the day. For instance, become aware of what happens when you're having a difficult conversation or delivering bad news. Is your feel space activated? Notice this and stay with it; don't distract yourself. In a meeting, is there a conversation going on in your head while others are speaking? If there is, you'll likely have missed what was said at the meeting. Have you ever noticed how many times people ask you to repeat what you just said, respond to something you never asked about, or change lanes while driving without checking their blind spot? All are clear signs that they were caught up in an internal story and not really present. By noticing what's going on internally when you're with others or driving, you'll become aware of how often you are in the present moment versus in your head, thinking about the past or future.

External Awareness

Being aware of what's going on around you also helps to train you to live in the present moment. Why is this important? Quite simply, it's only in the present moment that anything happens; everything else is either history or fantasy. It's the best way to enjoy a sunset, the company of your family, a golf game, a ski run, a business success . . . you get the idea. In addition, being in the present moment allows you to make clearer decisions, have better judgment, decrease your suffering, and experience greater fulfillment in life. Living in the present moment allows you to really hear what someone says when they speak, rather than what you wish they had said or what you fear they have said. This technique is especially useful in your conversations with your board, colleagues, staff, competitors, and family. External Awareness is an objective experience. If you're participating in a meeting with someone else who's being mindful, the likelihood is that you'll both see and hear very similar things.

Have you ever noticed how difficult it is to be in the present moment? Try looking at the palm of your hand and doing nothing else. Don't think about the hand, don't judge what you're doing, just focus on your hand. How long did your focus last before you became distracted? If you're like most people, it was probably only a few seconds. Why is this so hard? It's hard because an untrained mind experiences *monkey mind*. A monkey mind swings from one thing to another and then back again, relentlessly. In our culture, we turned this inability to concentrate into an erroneous interpretation of something positive, and called it multitasking. Multitasking is just an excuse that legitimizes our inability to concentrate. It's so ingrained in our culture that we've parlayed it into a desirable skill, but this couldn't be more mistaken and misguided.

In Chapter 2 I mentioned two significant studies. One indicated that those who multitask the most are the least competent at it. The other indicated that the average person in a workplace is interrupted every 11 minutes and it takes this same person, on average, 25 minutes to get back to the original task. With training, your ability to function in the present moment will enable you to refocus within seconds. Think of how productive, effective, and efficient companies would be if their people all had this ability. "The human brain, with its hundred billion neurons and hundreds of trillions of synaptic connections, is a cognitive power-house in many ways. But a core limitation is an inability to concentrate on two things at once," said René Marois, a neuroscientist and director of the Human Information Processing Laboratory at Vanderbilt University.[3] The implications are simple and clear: even if you're doing three things at the same time, only one thing can receive your attention in any given moment. This means that if you're checking your BlackBerry and participating in a meeting, one activity is being shortchanged. If you're talking or texting on your cell phone while driving, the likelihood of an accident is greatly increased. Evidence of this is so conclusive that many major cities have banned drivers from using handheld phones while behind the wheel. A recent U.S. study published in July 2009 by the Virginia Tech Transportation Institute found that "the risk of being involved in a safety-critical event—or risk of collision—was 23.2 times greater when drivers were texting than when they were not distracted."[4]

The reality is that the more you multitask, the less you're able to concentrate. Even if you're not interrupted by others, you'll begin to interrupt yourself. You may be thinking that you're far too busy to have the luxury of working on one project at a time or doing only one thing at a time. Remember that you can work on multiple projects without a problem, but only one in any given moment. By the end of the day you may have worked on four, five, or more projects, giving each one your undivided attention when you're working on it. This makes you more effective and efficient. You'll make fewer errors and gain greater satisfaction because you'll accomplish more. When you are able to focus this way you save time because you don't do anything twice.

Formal Technique

The concept in the External Awareness technique was popularized by Eckhart Tolle in his books *The Power of Now* and *A New Earth*; it will train you to be in the present moment. As with the technique of Internal Awareness, External Awareness encompasses three distinct spaces: *touch*, *sight*, and *sound*.

Touch space refers to your physical body and the sensations you experience. These sensations are not associated with emotion, as was the case with feel. Instead, touch is, for example, the sensation of the contact of your feet with the floor, of your clothing on your skin, of the breeze on your face. The body exists only in the present; it has no choice. Your body right now doesn't feel like it did a year ago, 10 years ago, or even 10 minutes ago. Nor does it feel the way it will tonight or next year. On the other hand, your mind does have a choice. It can live in the past, the future, and if trained, in the present moment.

Sight space refers to what you see when your eyes are open. It too exists only in the present moment. As any artist knows, the light changes throughout the day, producing differences in luminosity, creating different quality, shadows, and so on.

Sound space refers to what you hear in the outside world. This too occurs only in the present moment. The airplane that just went by is gone, the presentation you're listening to is only in the present. What the presenter said 15 minutes ago is gone; even if you ask him to repeat the exact same thing, it'll be a new sound—the old one is gone.

Just as with Internal Awareness, it's entirely possible that in a given moment you won't be aware of one of the three spaces because it's at rest. Remember that the state of all rest is when, and only when, all three spaces are at rest; if they're not, focus your attention on an active state.

This is a wonderful technique to work with in formal practice and in daily life. As a formal practice, sit in a chair or lie on the floor in a comfortable position and place awareness on your body; this is your touch space. Now, also place awareness on something you will softly gaze at. It can be a bowl in the center of a table, a tree outside the window, or anything you choose; this is your sight space. Be sure to continue to blink normally and to look at the entire object. Don't fixate on one particular part, as this may strain your eyes. Finally, place awareness on the sounds around you in the room, outside the room, and outside the building; this is your sound space.

Notice what comes into your awareness. You may become aware of one thing at a time or many things at once. Pick one to notice at a time. As with the Internal Awareness technique, notice what you become aware of, focus on it for a few seconds, and then move on to either notice the same thing again, if it's still there, or something different if it's not. For example, you may become aware of your feet touching the floor. Notice this, stay focused on it for a few seconds, and then become aware of what you're noticing now. It may be your feet again, or this time it may be the sound of voices outside. Stay focused on the sound of the voices, not to what's being said. After focusing for a few seconds, become aware again. This time you may become aware of the tree outside the window. Pay attention to sight for a few seconds, then continue the cycle. Find a comfortable rhythm and don't strain, just focus on what arises naturally. This will increase your concentration and create calmness. At first it may feel awkward, but keep at it and it will soon be quite pleasant and relaxing. Do this for at least 10 minutes at a time, ideally every day.

Strategies for Mindfulness in Action

In daily life, you will find that focusing on the present moment brings great fulfillment. Connect to your feet as you walk and you'll find you are quickly in touch with your body. Look at the sights and you'll find that you discover things you have never seen before, even on routes you have taken for years. Listen to the birds sing or go to a concert and truly listen to the music—it will sound magical. Listen to what's being said and you will be amazed at what you pick up.

The External Awareness technique can be used to great advantage in every aspect of business. I have used it successfully for years when negotiating strategic alliances. It enables you to have a keen awareness of leverage points and to determine how to relate to the people across from you at the negotiating table. It can also be used very effectively in sports. When you play any sport, connect with your body, the sights, and the sounds. If you're a runner, become aware of how your body moves as you run, and what you hear and see. If you play golf, be aware of your body as you address the ball, then just be present and swing. This is part of a more elaborate instruction, but you get the idea.

The task is simple: when you walk, walk; when you drive, drive; when having a conversation with someone, do nothing but speak or listen; when you eat, just eat; when you watch a sunset, just watch the sunset. Be fully present with whatever you are doing.

You might be thinking, "That sounds fine, but this leaves no room for planning or dealing with the future because it's not in the present." Of course, the answer to this is that you certainly can plan for the future in the present. All that matters is that when you're planning, that's all you're doing. Planning is conscious thinking, which is both useful and necessary.

Imagining Positive Outcomes

Imagining positive things is empowering. This is one of the reasons so many people enjoy daydreaming. We get to make up the fantasy and create the ending. Some of you may be surprised that there is a mindfulness technique where we do precisely this. It's a form of structured daydreaming called Creating or Imagining Positive Outcomes.

If you play competitive sports, you may recognize this as visualizing your perfect performance. Athletes have long experienced the benefit of training the body and the mind so they both function at peak performance. Phil Jackson, the NBA coach with the greatest number of NBA Championship titles, meditates before every game. Both Christopher Higgins and Mike Komisarek, formerly of the Montreal Canadiens hockey team, and now of the Vancouver Canucks and Toronto Maple Leafs respectively, use meditation as part of their training.

My experience with coaching athletes is that mindfulness is very effective as a way of creating calm and focus at will, as well as for visualizing their best performance. This is a powerful skill that can be translated into any aspect of life, whether preparing for a golf match, running a race, or giving a presentation. This can also be a useful technique when developing a vision for your business or your life purpose.

Formal Technique

This technique involves the same spaces that were introduced above in the Internal Awareness discussion. With that technique, you work with feel, image, and talk spaces without manipulating whatever arises. Now you're going to use the same spaces but this time also *create* feel, image, and talk.

Start by creating an image or images on the mental screen in front of or behind your closed eyes. For example, you can visualize yourself as being calm and relaxed. Then create your own mental talk that supports the image. You might say to yourself, "I am calm," repeating this over and over again at a leisurely pace. You may find that after a while you actually experience pleasant sensations, or *pleasant feel,* in the body. If that is the case, by all means encourage it to grow. Do this for at least 10 minutes a day, either while seated or lying down.

This technique generates confidence and can be very powerful in creating positive outcomes. It's also good for developing concentration.

Strategies for Mindfulness in Action

You can use this technique in daily life to help create your intentions, which can be powerful things. Always intend or visualize the positive; don't create negative self-talk. When you get up in the morning, you may wish to create an intention for the day. Think about what you would like to have happen. Before a meeting, spend a few minutes thinking about what your objectives are for the meeting.

There is a lot of truth in Napoleon Hill's words, "Whatever the mind can conceive and believe, it can achieve." The mind has a way of completing what we think about; just ask any golfers who have said to themselves, "Don't go in the water" or "Don't go in the sand." What do you think usually happens? More often than not, the ball lands in the water or the sand. Before negotiating a deal, intend to have a positive and mutually beneficial outcome. If you're concerned about your meeting with the analysts after a particularly difficult quarter, take a few moments before the meeting to imagine being calm and equanimous as you present your company's results, regardless of whether they are above or below expectation, and then go into the meeting with these images in your mind.

Train yourself to expect the best by imagining the best. And when you catch yourself in negative self-talk, take the time to notice it and create positive self-talk in its place.

You can apply the next two techniques in particular as you carry on the activities of your day both personally and professionally. The awareness that things are constantly changing and that we often experience uncertainty or not knowing is most evident in our daily lives. The following strategies can help you mindfully deal with these realities.

Constant Change

Nothing stays the same—we all know that. Thoughts change, feelings change, bodies change; in fact, change occurs moment by moment. Sometimes you perform well, sometimes you fall short despite every effort. Sometimes whatever you touch turns to gold, sometimes you can do no right. You win some, you lose some. It's just a fact of life. But whether something is positive or negative, one thing is for sure—it will pass. In fact, it's passing moment by moment. Knowing this and keeping perspective can help you to get over business challenges, disappointments, and family crises. It can also help to keep expectations realistic, such as remembering that growth can't go on forever, regardless of how good your products or services are or how exceptional your human capital.

Strategies for Mindfulness in Action

When things seem like they can't get any worse, proactively speak to yourself about maintaining the perspective that all things are in a constant state of change. Similarly, when your company stock is the darling of the investment community, maintain perspective and remember that this too will change. This may seem like a philosophical view, but it's a fact. This strategy in daily life is about maintaining perspective and enabling equanimity.

You may also wish to pay attention to how much changes around you moment by moment. Notice how your thoughts (image space and talk space) change, sometimes so much so that you can barely keep up. Note how you experience different sensations in the body (in both the touch and feel spaces). Listen to how the sounds change around you—singing birds at one moment, traffic the next, construction after that. As you drive, cycle, or walk along, notice how the sights change. It all changes, nothing stays the same.

Typically, we have the illusion that things stay the same because we play them back in our subjective spaces (feel, image, talk), but the reality is that very often the herd has moved, so to speak, and we haven't even noticed because we're locked in our minds. The memories you relive in your mind are constantly activating your feel space, which creates a mental loop and keeps you from being in the present moment.

Not Knowing (Don't Know)

The tendency for people is to want to know, to have answers for everything. We seek closure because that makes us comfortable. This often occurs when we prematurely create a strategic alliance with a less than ideal partner, or when we pretend to know the answer because we are embarrassed to be seen to know less than a colleague or staff member. If you really think about it, you'll see how little we actually control or know for certain. The drive to know and to have answers to everything is simply the result of a desire for control and our discomfort with not knowing.

Part of mindfulness is to become comfortable with not knowing (or "don't know")—you need to practice becoming comfortable with a mind that doesn't have all the answers. This will help you to widen the gap between stimulus and response, and you'll find that in that gap many answers will surface. To be okay with not knowing is to be comfortable in one's skin. There are many things in life that you can readily find answers for; that's what Google and Wikipedia are for. What I'm referring to is different. For example, you may be deciding whether to sell a business or merely restructure it. Sometimes the answer isn't immediately obvious, and you truly don't know what to do. In these instances it may be best to allow yourself to "not know" for a period, rather than forcing a decision because you can't bear not coming to a conclusion.

Strategies for Mindfulness in Action

How many times in your day do you not know the answer to something, and how does your mind react? Does it become desperate and try to grasp at some premature solution or response? This could occur anytime—when you're having conversations, in meetings, or deciding what projects to approve. For a day or two, just notice when this happens and do nothing about it. Simply observe yourself. Then, after a few days, when you have gotten into a rhythm of recognizing this in yourself, resist the temptation to find an immediate answer or premature closure. In the moment, try to not resist the not knowing; be equanimous with it and accept this confused state. Simply say to yourself, "Don't know," and be all right with it. Soon you'll notice that by allowing that gap to exist and to widen, answers are likely to arise more readily and your judgment will be more likely to improve.

The techniques I describe in this chapter are intended to form part of a regular, and preferably daily, practice and routine. Just 10 minutes per day has the potential to transform your life and make you a healthier, happier, and more effective person and leader. Feel free to take advantage of the audio recordings of guided meditations available at www.argonautaconsulting.com to guide you as you begin your meditation practice. I also encourage you to use the strategies for mindfulness in action so that you can experience even greater benefits. By doing both of these, you will experience greater mindfulness throughout the day in all aspects of your life. In time, you'll experience better control of your mind, so that your mind serves you and you gain more control of your life. This will enable you to maintain healthy and fulfilling relationships, personally and professionally, enabling you to be a *mindful leader.*

Chapter 4

Five Hindrances that Impede Success

Hindrances are mental states that impede success. They get in the way of you realizing your full potential as a leader and experiencing personal fulfillment, and they cause great suffering. There are numerous hindrances, but the five most applicable to our topic of mindful leadership are:

1. Attachment

2. Aversion

3. Ignorance, confusion, and delusion

4. Envy and jealousy

5. Pride

In the descriptions below, you'll see how these hindrances get in the way of being a mindful leader. They inhibit making good decisions, using good judgment, managing for performance, and winning in the marketplace, not to mention experiencing fulfillment in your life.

It's important not to judge yourself negatively if you recognize that you're experiencing, or have experienced, any (or all) of these hindrances. They're simply part of being human. Everyone experiences them in some form or other during their life. Sometimes all the hindrances may be evident at the same time; at other times, you'll be aware of only one or two. They ebb and flow and can be very intense or barely perceptible. These hindrances can also be interrelated. And if one manifests strongly enough, it may cause others to be activated.

Keep in mind that the hindrances are problematic only when they manifest in a dysfunctional way in your professional or personal life. If they begin to drive your behavior and cloud your focus, clarity, and equanimity (or acceptance of what's arising in your sensory experience—feel, image, and talk), you may need to address them and reexamine your priorities (more on how to do this later in the chapter). Working with hindrances is an ongoing process. If you recognize any of these in yourself, you can actively work with them moment by moment. I describe how to do this throughout the book.

It is also important to note that the same hindrances apply to both your personal and professional lives. Therefore, individuals, companies, and organizations are all affected by these hindrances. This should come as no surprise. After all, companies exhibit the patterns of their leaders and leadership teams. It is only from a place of equanimity that you can make the right decisions for yourself and for your organization.

The Hindrances

Attachment

Attachment refers to the unrelenting drive to succeed, to acquire, to compete, to control, and to the inability to let go.

This can apply to market standing, material goods, position, status, and even beliefs. Attachment is a fixation; you become convinced that you're absolutely correct in your views and desires, no matter what they are, and then you set out to create conditions that will support these views.

This explains, in part, why people acquire houses that are beyond their means, and yet they don't consider scaling back or modifying their lifestyle when they find that they can't pay the mortgage. Attachment causes the house itself to become a part of their identity. Without it, their view of themselves becomes unacceptable, as if the house makes them worthy and enhances their self-esteem and position in the world. The same applies when companies stretch themselves in ways they cannot afford. An acquisition may propel the company into greater market share, and maintaining this becomes an end in itself—whatever the price. At times, leaders may stay in a position too long. Often this is the result of being attached to the position or its associated status.

Attachment also explains how you can become fixated on the idea that your strategy is perfect as it is, even if consumer preferences have changed. You can become attached to the idea that somewhere there's a silver bullet, and if only you had a better team, better marketing, or better support, your company performance would improve markedly.

Aversion

Aversion is the fear of losing what you have, including market standing, material goods, financial resources, social position and status, or even an argument. You become so fearful of loss that you make poor decisions. As a leader, your aversion to bad news may tempt your team to withhold information from you or to paint a falsely rosy picture. Consequently, any decision you make may be based on erroneous or incomplete information, which will then combine with the next hindrance (ignorance, confusion, and delusion).

Aversion often expresses itself irrationally, blowing things out of proportion. A leader may see the company's stock price fall for a couple of weeks and be convinced of the need to completely change strategy. On a personal level, someone who's experiencing aversion in its extreme form might watch the stock market lose 500 points and immediately think that a market collapse is inevitable, or that another Great Depression is around the corner, and that he and his family will be destitute. If this reaction sounds far-fetched, believe me, it's not. I've worked with clients who could barely function in the fall of 2008 because they experienced such great anxiety from this aversion. It was only by tailoring mindfulness techniques to what they were experiencing, by using special exercises, and through their diligent practice that they were able to regain calmness and peace of mind.

Ignorance, Confusion, and Delusion

Together, ignorance, confusion, and delusion represent one hindrance. This hindrance is characterized by not seeing reality for what it is. Most people realize that they don't know what they don't know. However, those people with this hindrance believe they do know it all—often they're so sure that they're correct that it's impossible to convince them that they might actually not be.

Ignorance arises as a result of unfounded beliefs or views. It can also be indicative of a lack of clarity and a confused state of mind. An example of ignorance as a leader is assuming that "everyone negotiates the same way" when negotiating with others from a different culture.

Confusion is closely linked to ignorance and occurs when someone isn't fully aware of something, such as a leader receiving conflicting information from competing sources, particularly if he or she has a bias about the sources of the information.

Delusion refers to maintaining inappropriate patterns or not believing the facts because of particular biases. A deluded mind is often stuck in the past and uses the past to predict the future—an example of this is someone who believes she still holds the greatest brand or strategy, even though this is no longer the reality. A leader with a bias may refuse to see that a staff member they like is really not very competent and that the team has had to compensate for that person.

Like the other hindrances, the trio of ignorance, confusion, and delusion can cause great suffering when major events such as bankruptcy or restructuring occur. The saying "Ignorance is bliss" definitely has its limits.

Envy and Jealousy

Envy and jealousy are rooted in a place of deep insecurity and refer to wanting what others have. People who suffer from this hindrance feel that somehow they're not good enough, but that if they could just get what another person has, they'd be equally worthy. This "keeping up with the Joneses" mind-set presumes that self-esteem is inextricably linked with compensation, market success, material possessions, status, looks, or connections.

Envy and jealousy often manifest themselves through spending beyond one's means in order to buy another building, another company, a new computer system, a larger home, a boat, a second car. Or leaders may become envious that leaders in other companies receive higher compensation, believing that if their own salaries fall behind, they will not be as well perceived by the market or their peers. Leaders may become jealous if they see that a direct report is smarter or more likeable than they are. This is an indication that they are not secure within themselves.

When you fall victim to this hindrance, you feel a sense of incompleteness that you think can be relieved only by obtaining what someone else has or intends to have. But the satisfaction is fleeting, if it exists at all, because someone else always has more than you. As soon as you satisfy one desire, another creeps in and you're off in search of whatever will satisfy it, in a desperate attempt to maintain your sense of worthiness.

Envy and jealousy make you believe that satisfaction and fulfillment lie outside yourself, that by your nature you're incomplete and something external is required to make you whole. You can see how it's a slippery slope: much like an addict who is never satisfied, someone who is envious or jealous is never satisfied.

Pride

Pride manifests in two ways: as superior pride and as inferior pride. Superior pride says, "I am better than you"; inferior pride says, "You are better than me."

Those with superior pride need to win all the time in order to feel worthy. They'll go to great lengths to try to make others feel inferior—by reminding them of how smart they themselves are, how much money they have, how well connected they are, how successful their companies are, how much money they have made with their investments, even their golf handicaps. But it's all a bluff: in reality, sufferers of this hindrance are saying, almost with every breath, "I'm better than you, *aren't I?*"

Conversely, those with inferior pride believe they can do no right. They feel that everyone is more successful, smarter, faster, richer, luckier than them. They often think of themselves as situational victims. They too experience insatiability, but in their case it's insatiable inferiority. They often try to associate with those who have superior pride because by association they feel somewhat elevated in status. People with inferior pride tend to be copycats and follow trends for fear of being left behind or sticking out. They can be vulnerable to leadership fads or the latest hot trend.

Those who exhibit pride as a hindrance are often not coachable. They don't accept feedback about their leadership, and this will often lead to ineffectiveness or their demise as leaders.

Dealing with Hindrances

Everyone suffers from some of these hindrances from time to time. It's part of the human condition. However, if you find that you're so driven by any of these hindrances that it's affecting your ability to lead or your quality of life, then you may wish to implement some changes. If you recognize that you're suffering from some of these hindrances but they're not yet having an adverse affect on you, then simply being aware of this can be enough to keep you out of trouble. Remember that without awareness you lose options and are merely carried away by the moment: stimulus and response will have no gap, and you'll be forced to react rather than respond. I'm encouraging you to make good decisions, not to try to be perfect. Making good decisions can mean the difference between short-term gains and sustainable performance, between putting together a good team and putting together a great team.

Unchecked hindrances tend to move you away from focus, clarity, and equanimity. One of the benefits of practicing mindfulness is that these hindrances, over time, begin to dissolve and eventually can wash away altogether. In Chapter 2 I introduced the concept of purification. Hindrances are some of the patterns that can be purified by regular meditation practice. When you look back on things after practicing for some time, you'll find that the things that really used to bother or worry you no longer have a hold on you at all. You'll wonder what's happened—you've practiced and maybe felt a little calmer and more at peace but believed nothing unusual happened in your practice. However, in hindsight, you'll see how your life has been transformed.

As you continue practicing, you'll increasingly find that you're no longer driven. Rather, you're *motivated*. Motivated to do things, to accomplish your goals. You're no less effective with this lack of drive—drive is generally associated with an insatiable craving that, over time, takes control over your mind. Motivation, on the other hand, keeps you focused toward and engaged in your goals and inspired to achieve them. In fact, being motivated, you'll be more effective because you'll be focused on what you want to achieve, clear about what you want to achieve, and equanimous (calmly accepting) about the outcome. Concerned that a lack of drive will make you less competitive and effective? Just observe Phil Jackson, coach of the Los Angeles Lakers, and you'll see just how effective you can be without being slavish. His meditation practice helps the team to stay motivated to succeed rather than being driven to it. They know that if they focus on playing the best game possible rather than on the score, the score really will take care of itself.

Remember that you can influence your behavior but not your results; trying to control situations usually backfires, and they end up controlling you. When you're fixated on controlling outcomes, you miss opportunities. You get stuck in the past or the future and don't function with ease in the present moment—the only moment that truly exists. If you take care of this moment, of performing in it, the next one will take care of itself.

This is no different from creating a business plan that's in line with your vision, mission, and strategy while staying actively focused, clear, and equanimous (balanced, rather than fighting with yourself), regardless of external influences, like a key competitor's product launch, for instance. When you're mindful, you become aware of when you need to alter the strategic course and you remember how and when to seek advice. You are likely to make better decisions. Unencumbered by worry or fear, you can respond with agility when required and stay put when required. Rather than being influenced by the herd, you're guided by your internal compass.

Mindful Exercise

Here is a useful meditation exercise when you want to reflect upon any of the hindrances described above and what part they play in your life. Begin by relaxing yourself to the best of your ability (you may wish to use the techniques described in Chapter 3). Then ask yourself some or all of the following questions, reflecting on one or even two questions at a time:

- Is there anything that you're attached to, so much so that you say to yourself, "I won't/can't let go of this, no matter what"? It could be a position, a possession, a belief, or something else. You may feel so attached to it that you think, "If I were to lose X, I'd be devastated."

- Is there anything that you have a deep aversion to? The aversion could take the form of a huge fear or a significant worry. It might be an aversion to not meeting analyst expectations of earnings per share or to losing market share, or it could be an aversion to your children not following the family tradition of becoming whatever (name the profession), or to losing money in your investment portfolio.

- Has someone you respect ever told you that you're not thinking clearly or that you're not basing your decisions on facts? This may be a sign that you're suffering from ignorance, confusion, and delusion. This hindrance can manifest in the belief that since you tried X a number of years ago and it didn't work, it won't work now.

- Do you ever experience envy and jealousy to the point where you purchase or do something just because someone else does? Take the time to think about why you did it, especially if it really wasn't what you wanted. Have you ever released a product prematurely or entered a market because a competitor did? Have you ever gone into debt because you were trying to keep up with someone else?

- Are you constantly comparing yourself with others? Do you need the approval of others to feel worthy? Do you need to be with others who may appear inferior to you in order to feel at ease or, conversely, who you believe to be superior to you in order to draft off their elevated status? Do you constantly compare your compensation as a leader with that of others, so much so that it impacts how you feel about what you do and where you do it?

In addition to reflecting upon these thoughts in meditation, try being aware during the course of your day. Begin by choosing one hindrance for a week, or even for just a couple of days, and try to become aware when you exhibit it. For example, become aware when and where you exhibit attachment. It could be in your professional life, at home, or on the golf course. Do nothing about what you discover; simply become aware of it. Your goal is to increase the awareness in your day-to-day life. Pay particular attention when you are in a position to influence another person. Are you doing this from a place of authenticity and service, or does it come from a hindrance? What is your relationship to money, whether it be your own or your company's? Money is an important litmus test. Very often, if you can be clear about money, you can be clear about a lot of other aspects of your life.

If you want to take it a step further, pay attention to what's happening in your subjective world (your feel, image, and talk spaces) when you experience any of the hindrances very strongly. For example, if you experience great jealousy, make contact with your feel space and locate the jealousy in your body. Is there an image on your mental screen? Is there some commentary in the talk space? As you know from Chapter 3, you want to stay focused and concentrate on what's going on. You want to be clear and notice what's arising in your sensory experience, and you want to surrender to it. In other words, you want to be equanimous. Don't resist it, because resisting can take the form of judging or justifying yourself. Do neither of these; just stay with it and have a full experience. This is how purification occurs.

To reiterate, the goal is not to become perfect and free from all of the hindrances. Rather, you should be interested in experiencing life fully; finding fulfillment; and minimizing, if not eliminating, suffering. Any of the hindrances that are allowed to go unchecked and get out of control can cause great suffering to both you and those around you. As a leader, you have the potential to impact many people. Being aware of your hindrances is critical to understanding your reactions toward others as well as the impact you have on them. The hindrances also prevent you from finding fulfillment in life, since they cause you to live primarily, if not exclusively, in the past and the future. Fulfillment occurs only in the present.

By doing this exercise as both a formal practice and as a strategy for mindfulness in action, you can accelerate and deepen your mindfulness skills.

Chapter 5

Discovering Your Life Purpose

As human beings we are constantly asking questions. One of the deepest questions we ask is, "What is my life purpose?" At the root of it, we want to know why we are here. We want to know that all of our efforts in this life are not in vain—that our lives have meaning and purpose. However, most people have no idea why they are on this earth. Not knowing your life's purpose is not limited by socioeconomic group, level of education, age, gender, or culture. It appears to cut across all boundaries.

Most of the people I have worked with are searching for the same answers. When pressed, people usually will say they're here to be a good mother, father, daughter, son, sibling, friend, and so on. That they're here to lead the company to success, to help develop useful products, to be a good teacher, doctor, lawyer, leader.

You'll notice that their responses are all centered on roles. Unfortunately, when you see your life in terms of roles, you can't help but falter. The hindrances will rear their ugly heads. People may become attached to their roles, averse to losing them, deluded about how much control they have, or envious of those with more prestigious roles, or they may feel inferior or superior pride in relation to others.

This is a slippery slope. For people who give these roles such importance, if any or all of them don't go well, are lost, or are negatively judged by others, it impacts their sense of worth, even their sense of self. Pretty soon they start behaving in ways that they think will receive approval or that will cause them to be well regarded.

You can probably see where this is leading. If people spend a lifetime seeking approval, or at the very least seeking not to be rejected, they'll eventually find themselves not knowing what they want, enjoy, or value. They start living someone else's life, perhaps one that represents parents' or siblings' or society's ideals. They try to live up to a standard they have interpreted as being worthy. I see this all the time—people who decide to head up the family business even though they have no interest in doing so, or those who became doctors or lawyers because their parents had that profession or wanted to have it. The kids are living their parents' dreams but not their own. Alternatively, some people pick professions or roles that they think will give them security. This may turn out positively if what they choose is in line with their own interests. But if it's not, the end result may be the same as living a life they allowed someone else to choose for them.

If, after years of doing what you don't enjoy, you are faced with an opportunity to do something different—either because you are financially comfortable and can afford to do so or because you have lost your job—you may have no idea what to do, nor how to go about figuring out what to do. Many people who come to see me are precisely in this position. Many are highly successful and accomplished at what they do, but they do not experience fulfillment. They sense that something is missing.

Essentially what they experience at this point is a crisis of spirit. They wonder what life is all about. The crisis can manifest as a sense that life has no meaning; of course it can feel that way if you are living someone else's expectations. Or they erroneously fall into the trap of believing that more is better—more money, a more senior position, more direct reports, a bigger house—in essence, more status and more stuff. This is a malaise of our time. Wherever you see a constant striving for more, you will find lack of fulfillment. This is merely a search for meaning in all the wrong places. This is a craving, an attachment (the first hindrance). Twenty-five hundred years ago, the Buddha called it the root of all suffering.

And what is the antidote to this? It's really quite simple: to get to know yourself deeply, to know who and what you are. And that is where mindfulness comes in. Mindfulness training enables you, with practice, to arrive at that very place where you know beyond a shadow of a doubt that you are a spiritual being in a human existence. And knowing this deeply makes you a better human. It gives you purpose. You quickly come to a place where you know that ultimately you are here to be of service. The more you refine consciousness, the more this becomes self-evident.

Being of service has grown to be cliché. It's spoken of in terms of serving clients, constituents, et cetera—essentially being of service to those who pay us or vote for us. But it is much broader than that. It literally means being of service in the world for the benefit of all beings. And now you might say, "If I am busy being of service to everyone else, where do I fit in?" The irony is that when you are of service to others, you automatically best serve yourself.

As leaders, we are here to serve all those we have the opportunity to influence. Leadership carries with it great privilege and great responsibility. And you would be hard-pressed not to see how each and every one of us is a leader. Every day, in some big and many small ways, we have the opportunity to influence another being. What we do with that opportunity can change the course of someone's life. So a leader is not exclusively someone with formal authority, but each and every person who is in a position, however briefly, to influence another. Is there anyone in your organization, your family, your community who is not in that position each and every day?

You might be thinking, "But surely the leadership requirements for someone who leads a global enterprise are different from those of someone interacting with a person at the checkout counter." While the content of the requirements is certainly different for each of these individuals, the activity of leadership is identical—it doesn't matter whether you are influencing millions of people or just one at any given moment. There will be much more on this in the chapters to come.

Until you know who and what you are, you'll experience a general malaise, a sense of incompleteness. In my twenties I had a deep yearning and a general sense of uneasiness. Personally and professionally I had great success by all external measures. But I knew there was something missing. I knew I had a purpose in this life, but I didn't know what it was. This caused me great angst. This is how I came to practice mindfulness. Through serendipity I came across my first teacher. In time, with a great deal of practice and good training, my purpose unfolded and became clear. And that vision for my life has guided me through the decades.

Through mindfulness training you become intimately familiar with what motivates you, what makes you happy, what you fear, what you hope for—essentially what makes you tick. It is a journey to become intimately acquainted with yourself. It's a journey back to where you started, and as T.S. Eliot puts it, "to know the place for the first time." Remember that as a young kid, before you took on other people's desires, you had some pretty well-defined interests. Most of us were partial to certain play or certain activities. Those were the times when we lost ourselves and had to be called home for dinner because we had lost track of time.

That's what you are after in discovering your life purpose. Those experiences and activities that make you lose yourself. And there is a fairly simple and easy way to discover your life purpose. It just takes some work, reflection, and a willingness to be open and amaze yourself. It also requires a willingness to listen to yourself and not shut yourself down because what you come up with is not what someone else's voice has said in your head your whole life.

The process of completing the reflective exercises described below will help you arrive at awareness of your life purpose. In completing the various reflective exercises, some of you may come up with a concrete life purpose, for others it will be the beginning of a meaningful journey to get to know the most important person in your life—you.

I have used this process with many businesspeople and professionals, both on a one-on-one coaching basis and in workshops, and it is remarkably effective and efficient. Take time to reflect and to refine your answers over days and weeks. And know that it is one of the most worthwhile things you will ever do for yourself.

Reflective Exercises

Start by carving out some time for yourself. You can begin with an hour or so, or you may be the kind of person who wishes to do the exercises all in one or two longer stretches. When I coach someone individually through the process, we work through it over several weeks and intertwine it with special mindfulness exercises tailored to that person's needs. In a workshop setting, I work through it over a day and a half, meditating and reflecting in a particular sequence. You are the best judge of what works for you.

Step 1

Start by sitting quietly, ideally in a comfortable place where you won't be disturbed, and allowing yourself to be still to the best of your ability. You may wish to do the relaxation meditations described in Chapter 3 or listen to the guided relaxation meditations on my website at www.argonautaconsulting.com to help you get into the proper frame of mind.

Step 2

Examine your entire life, from your earliest memories. Focus on times when you were happy, joyful, or at peace, and when you felt successful. Just do some brainstorming—don't censure yourself or discount anything. In fact, your first thoughts will be very revealing. Do not do any analysis at this time. Here you are only interested in capturing whatever comes to mind.

Write everything down, because as you move through the process you will be looking for patterns. Here are questions to consider:

- What were you doing?
- Were you with others?
- What were the circumstances?
- What was the environment like?
- What did it feel like?

Step 3

Now is the time for analysis. Examine what it was about these times that was joyful. Analyze the memories and look for common characteristics. Ask yourself the following questions:

- Were you using certain skills?
- Was there something particular about the environment?
- Was there something particular about the people? What were their personal characteristics? Were they kind, humorous, clear, et cetera?

Step 4

You have covered a lot of ground by this point. Steps 2 and 3 require that you systematically reflect on your entire life, examining all the high points. This is a detailed process.

Once you have completed Steps 2 and 3 to your satisfaction, take a break. Walk around, stretch, whatever suits your needs at the time, and allow what you have been thinking about to sink in. This is a deliberate step because the process of mental integration is important.

Step 5

This step is a formal meditation. You can use a relaxation technique once again as in Step 1, or you may wish to work with either the Internal Awareness or External Awareness technique, described in detail in Chapter 3. If there is a significant amount of emotion in the thinking mind and feeling body, you may wish to work with Internal Awareness. If you are tense, work with relaxation. Otherwise, just be with the simplicity of the present moment by working with External Awareness.

Step 6

Now you are going to change gears. Systematically go through your life again from your earliest memory, only this time reflect on when you were least happy, when life seemed like a struggle, and when you experienced little or no inner peace. You may have experienced deep unhappiness or you may have just had persistent, low-grade dissatisfaction. If you find yourself saying,

"But everything seemed so perfect, why was I so miserable?" or if you remember asking yourself, "Is this all there is?" then you know you have hit upon an important time. Write everything down so it will be available for analysis in Step 7. Ask yourself these questions:

- What were you doing?

- What was the environment like?

- What were the personal characteristics of the person or people involved? Were they uncommunicative, harsh, distant, et cetera?

- What did you experience?

As in Step 2, this is just information gathering. Do not explain, rationalize, dismiss, or justify. You may be surprised at what you come up with. Some unhappy periods seem very obvious, but others may not be as evident.

Step 7

Now is the time to analyze. What was it about these times that made you so unhappy and ill at ease? Ask yourself these questions:

- Were you using skills you didn't enjoy using?

- Were you in an environment that made you uncomfortable?

- Were you working with people you didn't enjoy being with? Or were you not working with others? Was it a solitary job, or was there too much interaction or stimulation for your liking?

Give yourself time to really reflect. Some of your responses and memories may be painful. Honor that, and don't dismiss how they make you feel. There can be great learning in staying with what makes you uncomfortable.

Once you've completed this step, take a break. You can choose to continue the same day, after a good, long break, or on another day.

Step 8

Now you are going to work with the hindrances—attachment; aversion; ignorance, confusion, delusion; envy and jealousy; and pride (discussed in Chapter 4). Follow these four steps:

1. Review your happiest times. Were there any hindrances at play? If you experienced hindrances, what were they?

2. Now review your unhappiest times. Were there any hindrances at play? In all likelihood there were one or more. What were they?

3. Now examine your life at the present moment. Are there hindrances at play in your life right now? How do they manifest?

4. Review your responses to the above three steps. Can you discern a pattern? Are there hindrances that have been evident your entire life, or are new ones cropping up?

To experience real freedom, you need to purify your hindrances. (See Chapter 2, page 18, for a description of purification.) Real freedom is freedom from the tyranny of your thinking mind and feeling body. When these go unchecked, they drive behavior, causing repetitive negative patterns. The way in which these patterns are dissolved is through meditation practice. By using the techniques described in Chapter 3, you can become intimately familiar with what motivates you. By so doing, you are best able to divide and conquer what is arising within you so that you don't blindly react but, instead, respond to circumstances.

Step 9

Now you're going to change gears again. Picture this: You have reached the end of a highly fulfilling life. You are a wise, old being. What has your life been like? Consider the following:

- What kind of person are you?

- What have you achieved?

- What experiences have you had?

- What are your hobbies? How did you spend your leisure time?

- What is the state of your spiritual life?

- What and how have you given back?

Write a description for yourself that summarizes what you imagine your life will have been like.

Step 10

Now you are going to write out a vision for your life. A vision underpins everything. It is a generic statement that will be a guiding force in your life. Creating a personal vision is exactly the same as creating a vision for your company or institution. A well-run organization has a clear vision and strategy. In fact, without vision, mission, and strategy, companies flounder. They are pulled in every direction, enter markets for which they are ill-suited, launch products that are not in line with their core competencies, and acquire business that causes them to lose their focus.

The same is true if you don't have a personal vision and strategies to make that vision a reality. As a leader, having a clearly defined personal vision will enable you to know what roles to pursue, how long to stay in them, and how you can best contribute.

My personal vision statement has evolved over the decades, but fundamentally it has not changed. It is "to enable and empower others to reach their full potential by helping them discover the wisdom within." This vision applies to anything I do professionally and in my personal life.

A personal vision can be used to assess all major decisions in your life, to decide if an opportunity is worth seeking, and to determine if you are spending your time wisely. It becomes the litmus test for everything. If an opportunity is not in line with your vision, you then have a decision to make. But at least you will be doing it with your eyes wide open.

Do not try to craft a perfectly worded vision at the outset. Start by getting the concept right. Then you can work on crafting the words that you will be most comfortable with. As long as the intent is there, the words are likely to flow.

You may have crafted or contributed to crafting your company's vision, and you know that was a work in progress.

Take your time and have fun with it. It is one of the most worthwhile exercises you will do in your life.

Step 11

Now it's time to answer three important questions. These will help guide your life choices:

1. What would you do if you knew you could not fail?

2. What would you do if there was no judge or jury—if you did not judge yourself and no one else judged you?

3. What would you do if money was not an issue?

The answers to these questions can be very revealing. The idea here is not to censure yourself. Do not discount anything that comes to mind or judge it negatively because you don't think it's realistic or possible. As Napoleon Hill, American author of *Think and Grow Rich*, points out, the reality is that "whatever the mind can conceive and believe, it can achieve."[1] Intention is a very powerful force in our lives.

If you find yourself saying, "Yes, but . . .," see if there are any hindrances that are causing you to say this (you may wish to refer to Chapter 4 to help you with this). Once you become aware of a hindrance, work with the Internal Awareness technique to help you process what is arising within you so that you will not be driven by your feel space without realizing how and why you made a certain choice or decision. At least now you have choices by having greater awareness.

Step 12

Working with your vision, the guiding force in your life, develop your mission, which is essentially a plan for realizing your vision. My suggestion is that you select three time frames to work with, perhaps 6 months, 12 months, and somewhere between two and five years.

Write out for yourself what you will need to do in the next 6 months to move you in the direction of your vision, so that when it's time to pass on, you will have had a fulfilling life, one that mattered to you. What will you need to do in 12 months? And what will you need to do in two to five years?

The time frames should be updated periodically so that they are valid throughout your life. At any point in your life you should be looking at least two years out, perhaps further if you are so inclined.

This is the process I use with companies developing their corporate strategies, but it applies equally to your personal life. It is from this core that you can effectively move out into the world and make a difference, regardless of your age or stage of life.

If you are in your fifties or sixties and think it's too late for you to put everything in place in your working life, think again. Every moment is a new moment. You will be amazed at what can unfold for you in a very short period when you are focused with a clear intention. And if you are in your twenties and think you have lots of time, think again. Life goes by in a flash. You have the luxury of starting early; don't waste it. I developed my first vision statement in my early twenties, and it was one of the most important things I have ever done.

Give yourself the time you need to discover your life purpose. Deep within, your wisdom knows exactly why you're here.

Part 2

Mindful Leadership

Chapter 6

Be Present

Being present is the starting point of being a mindful leader. Essentially, this means being in the present moment regardless of circumstances. Most people are locked in their minds and unable to give full attention to what's happening right now. They are either reliving the past, wishing it had been different, or experiencing anxiety about the future, worrying about what might be. But both of these waste time and energy.

The reality is, the past is gone, never to be recaptured or corrected, and the future has not yet happened. The past is merely a memory and, in all likelihood, not a very accurate one at that. And you may have noticed that most of the things you have worried about in your life have never happened. But, typically, you don't notice they haven't happened because as soon as that worry is gone, you're on to the next one. Worry is a habit of the mind. The more you worry, the deeper the habit. In some people, worry can also be a form of superstition—that is, if you worry, you are somehow warding off the possibility of something going wrong. But we know that logically this is faulty thinking.

Have you ever noticed that if five people experience a situation, there will be five versions of what took place? How could that be? They were all there. But were they really? If those present have not trained their minds to be in the present moment, they are unlikely to be, and certainly won't be for any significant period. Instead, they are reliving or recreating the past or fantasizing about the future.

Combine this lack of focus with the fact that we experience reality based on our biases, judgments, patterns, and hindrances, and it is no surprise that we have misunderstandings in so many interactions in our professional and personal lives. Every situation can be improved if the participants are fully present. In fact, being present is the greatest gift you can give another person. When you are right here right now, you see things for what they really are. Often the reason we leave the present moment is because we have a disagreement with it, we are not okay with what is. We would prefer that it be another way. This resistance, or lack of equanimity with the present moment, leads to problems for us and others.

But the reality is that life happens right now only. If you are not present, you have missed life and will never recapture that loss. Inattention can mean you miss hearing what was said at a meeting or seeing the expression on the face of someone you love. And like every skill, the less we practice it, the less we are able to do it—to the point where there comes a time when we cannot have presence of mind despite our efforts.

Mindful Interactions

When you are present, you are able to have mindful interactions throughout your day, and these are critical to your success as a leader. People look to see if their leaders are truly there or just faking it. When you are "not there," people will interpret according to their own biases. They may think you don't agree with them, or that what they are saying is not important, or, worse, that they are not important. Picture this: You are in a business planning meeting, and rather than listening to someone's presentation with undivided attention, you are looking at your BlackBerry or excusing yourself to take calls. What does that signal to the presenter and others in the meeting? In its extreme, the interpretation could be "My division is in trouble" or "I am no longer a valued member of the team." This sentiment is not likely to generate the best performance from your team.

Now picture listening intently. Listening intently actually prompts the person who is speaking to be on his or her toes. It puts you in a position to ask pertinent questions. And the more skilled you become at being present, the more you hone your intuition and know what to ask and when to ask it. You can tell if someone is withholding information or just not adequately prepared. And it does not come from your biases but from seeing things as they really are.

Being a mindful listener simply means that when you are in a position to listen, you are completely listening to and observing the speaker and the reaction of others to the speaker and to what is being said. Truly being present like this makes you more effective and efficient. One thing that mindful people often report is that meetings take significantly less time than they once did. For example, as a mindful listener you are less likely to require others to repeat themselves. And because you've been listening, you know the facts and you can make appropriate decisions in a timely manner.

Being a mindful speaker means that you stick to the point and stay on message, while observing how others are taking in what you are communicating. By observing as you speak, you are able to clarify on the spot if required. You are able to see if you have buy-in and where and who your greatest challenges are likely to be. When you are in a position to speak, speaking mindfully means you say only what is necessary—no more, no less. You say what you mean and you mean what you say. You will notice that when people do not speak mindfully, they ramble, they repeat themselves, and they go off on tangents. Sometimes they might even say, "Where was I going with that?"

Mindful listening and mindful speech are among the most valuable skills to develop and cultivate as a leader. Let's return to the example of participating in a meeting. (The same would, of course, apply if you were having a conversation with your partner or a friend, say, or a child.) If you are in a position to listen, use both sound and sight. Listen to the words, tone, inflection, and conviction. Watch the body language of the speaker and the audience. By combining both sound and sight, you will not only pick up the content of what is being com-municated but will also develop your intuition, which will enable you to pick up what is *not* said too. This in turn enables you to ask questions and probe at the right moment, so that you have the clearest and most accurate understanding of what the communicator really means. This is very helpful, because many people do not communicate clearly.

If you catch your thoughts wandering off as you try to listen mindfully, very gently bring yourself back. This is about training your mind to be in the present moment. You may need to do this dozens or even hundreds of times. "Wandering off" can refer to being distracted and thinking about your next meeting or your tee-off time, or it can refer to getting caught up in your judgments, thinking of what you will say next, or dismissing what is said because you don't agree. In all cases, just come right back. Be patient with yourself and be persistent. One thing my clients consistently report is that when they and their teams work in this way, there are fewer interruptions and team members don't cut one another off or finish others' sentences.

Mindful speech refers to being very aware of the way in which you communicate. One of the most effective ways of training yourself to speak mindfully is to listen to the sound of your own voice. At first this can seem odd and a little uncomfortable, almost the way it felt when you heard your voice recorded for the first time. But it is incredibly effective in helping you stay on message. You will find that in time it will help you to speak from a place of wisdom. The voice of wisdom or presence sounds very different from a regular voice that is not speaking mindfully. There is a quality of sincerity and openness to the voice. If you start to ramble or go off message or topic, you will notice right away and you can just come right back to the present moment.

When you first practice mindful speech, it may appear that it's all you can do—it seems to take all your energy and focus. However, it will become easier. In time you will notice that you are very aware of others in the room and how your message is being perceived and interpreted. You will see who is buying-in and who is doubtful or uncommitted. In conversation with someone you will notice how what you are saying and how you are saying it is impacting that person.

Mindful listening and speaking are very powerful ways to communicate and can reduce or eliminate misunderstandings. My experience is that, where mindful listening and speaking are practiced, meetings and the overall work environment are more relaxed, open, and productive, engendering greater trust among employees because they know everyone will be heard. This does not mean that everyone agrees. What it does mean is that everyone's views are respected and heard. When this happens, disagreements are less likely to be taken personally because the focus is on what is said, not on who is saying it. On a personal level, mindful communication enables those you interact with to know that you accept them and love them unconditionally. What they say will be heard with little or no judgment. It creates the opportunity to hear things that may normally be withheld or sugarcoated. Overall it makes for deeper, more authentic relationships.

You can see how being a mindful listener and mindful speaker applies to every aspect of leadership, professionally and personally. Whether you are making a board presentation, meeting with the analyst community, listening to clients, managing conflict, doing a performance review, mentoring a member of your team, or developing strategy, developing your ability to be present is critical.

MINDFUL MAKEOVER

The Scenario

You are on the phone with your biggest customer, who is unhappy, and you think you may lose this key account.

Before

A common reaction is to become fearful that you will lose your biggest customer. As this thought enters your mind, you stop listening to what he is telling you. Instead, you think about what losing the account will do to your numbers and your reputation, and how it will be impossible to make up the financial loss in the short term, and you worry that you may never be able to make this shortfall up in a competitive market.

No matter how long your customer speaks, you won't hear anything he says. You'll be locked in your mind and not in the moment. The client doesn't feel listened to—because you're not listening.

After

A mindful leader hears exactly what is being said. You are present and stay in the moment. You understand that your biggest customer is extremely dissatisfied and that you are at risk of losing the account. You use mindful listening so that you hear his words and tone. You are so present that you hear what is being

(continued)

said and also, potentially, what is intended but not articulated. You also use mindful speech so that you can clarify what you are hearing. You hear your own voice and know, moment by moment, if it has an edge, if you are staying on message, if you are being defensive.

Rather than getting lost in your worries and missing what your client is saying, you have a mindful conversation. This means you can pick up what is truly bothering the client, and you can identify opportunities for corrective action. The only way you can effectively do this is by being fully present.

External Awareness

You can train yourself in a systematic way to be present. In Chapter 3 I talked about a technique called External Awareness (review that chapter for the specific details of the technique). It involves being aware of three things: your body, the sights you can see, and the sounds you can hear.

The Body

The body exists only in the present. Any concept that you have of how your body once felt is memory; any concept of how it will feel in the future is a projection or fantasy. Right here right now is all there is. That is why the body is so helpful in bringing you back to the present moment. It is a gift as close as your fingertips or your breath. The breath is another way of becoming aware of your body in the present moment. You breathe in and breathe out and you are right here.

Sight

What you can see with your eyes open exists only in the present. If you recall where people were seated at a meeting after the meeting is over, that is no longer sight; that is a memory, an image in your mind's eye. As every artist knows, even if you stay in the same place, moment by moment the light is changing. A canvas painted at 9 a.m. in one location will look quite different from one painted at 3 p.m. in the same location. Sight exists only in the present.

Sound

Sound too exists only in the present. If you are listening to someone speak or listening to a beautiful piece of music, it's happening right here and now. If later you replay the person's words in your mind or are playing the music in your head, that too is a memory and is considered internal talk.

Remember, the objective is not to become skilled at formal meditation for its own sake. The true prize is in being able to be mindful moment by moment as you move through your day, whether you are in a critical meeting, walking down the street, on the golf course, on a treadmill, or playing ball with your child.

Strategies for Mindfulness in Action

In order to be more and more mindful, you need to train yourself throughout the day. I have found that the clients I coach make tremendous progress when they actively work with mindfulness-in-action strategies. I discussed this briefly in Chapter 3 and will go into more detail here using various examples.

There is the opportunity for mindful listening and mindful speaking for a large part of your waking hours. That is why I consider mindful listening and mindful speaking to be the cornerstone of developing the skill of being present. In addition to interacting with people, opportunities for being present include walking down the street, driving a car, working out, listening to music, playing a game of bridge, tennis, or a round of golf.

For example, as you walk down the street, become aware of your body. Notice how your feet touch the ground, how your arms swing at your sides, how the air feels on your face. Now become aware of what you see. (After doing this, many people report noticing buildings and details they completely missed for years.) Finally, tune in to what you hear. It may be the sounds of birds as you walk through a park or the sounds of the city, including the honking of cars. There is a sense of aliveness when you are present as you walk.

Driving is also an excellent way to practice being present. Become aware of the contour of your body in the seat, your hands on the steering wheel—this is your body in that present moment. Now become aware of what you see in front of you, in your periphery, in the rearview mirror. Listen to the sounds of the traffic, music, or voices on the radio. Working with the three areas of focus—your body, sights, and sounds—is the safest way to drive because you are completely aware of what is arising in the moment. It enables you to more effectively anticipate some of the mindless driving we are all subjected to. And it may help prevent an accident. What you will find when you are driving mindfully is that you are more likely to arrive at your destination relaxed rather than tense. And if you spend a great deal of your time on the road, it is a wonderful opportunity to practice mindfulness in action and hone your skill by training your mind.

The same applies when you are working out. Become completely aware of how your muscles feel as you lift the weights or as you run. The body is a real miracle, and to be conscious of how you are working with it and developing it can be truly satisfying. By being present when you lift a weight, for instance, you are more able to judge if the weight is too light, too heavy, or just right for that particular work-out. You no longer exercise by rote, but rather by being in constant dialogue with your body and its needs—not what your mind or ego want. And if you think you need a break from that much focus on your body as you work out, be aware of the body sufficiently so that you do not cause any harm. If you are running outside, be aware of the sights and the sounds around you. If indoors, perhaps you can enjoy some music you really love.

Mindfulness is critical in playing golf, tennis, soccer, running a marathon, or participating in any other sport, and is a broad subject encompassing various techniques. But suffice to say here that you are likely to consistently perform better when you are present. You'll derive the greatest pleasure because you'll be able to enjoy your good shots or passes and not let your bad shots or misses dictate the rest of the round or game. You'll learn that once a shot or kick is over, it's over, and you'll be able to move on to your next shot or the next pass. This way you start fresh each moment, and your body is more likely to be relaxed.

Often when people first start to work with me, they ask why being present matters. They ask because they do some of their best thinking when they walk or when they drive, and they don't think they can afford to give up this time to be present. They are also concerned that if they focus only on the present, they will be unable to plan for the future. These are valid and legitimate concerns and come from a place of incomplete understanding about what it means to be mindful or present. Mindfulness is about being conscious, awake in the moment, no matter what you are doing. So when you are planning, you plan for the future—in the present without distractions. It makes you better able to plan. If you are walking and wish to think, that is a conscious act. You have made a decision to think. That is fine. I'm not trying to eliminate thinking per se; I merely want you to be conscious about what you're doing. So when you wish to think, think; when you wish to walk, walk; and when you decide to plan, plan. You will find that by being conscious you are much more effective and efficient. Eventually, with practice, you will find that you don't do anything twice. This will give you extra time, to do with as you choose.

Thinking itself is not the enemy as long as it is a conscious decision. It only becomes a problem when it happens all day— when you find that an hour has gone by and you have been lost in thought, either gripped by the past or worrying about the future, and you have not heard what others have said to you or noticed that your child has just scored a goal. Unless you train yourself to be in the present moment, you will find it harder and harder to be present. Without training your mind, you have less and less choice to be present. Again, this is about training your mind so that it does not control you.

Another thing that you will notice as you become more present is that you will think less, but the right answers and opportunities will come to you more readily. Eventually, you'll live from a place of intuition, a place of wisdom. Now, if this statement strikes you as going too far, think about the last time you had a truly brilliant thought or resolved a really tough issue. Did you actually think your way through it or did it arise spontaneously, almost out of nowhere? Most people will report that they were in the shower or walking down the street when the answer just came to them. That is what I am referring to. With training you will be more and more able to do this at will. What needs to be said comes out at the right time because you are so present that "you" are actually absent. In fact, that is how I wrote this book. It is about eventually living in a state of grace. We all have vast reservoirs—in fact, infinite reservoirs—of wisdom, and the more present you are, the more you are able to tap into this wisdom. But doing so requires training. Everyone is capable of this; it just takes motivation and good techniques—and the mindfulness-in-action strategies are very effective and quick ways to train.

Chapter 7

Be Aware

Being aware has many layers, but it begins with being self-aware. This means that you are aware of your thoughts and feelings moment by moment. You are aware of how different people and situations affect you. You are aware of how the hindrances manifest in your life, both personally and professionally. It also means that you are aware of how you impact others; how your words, your actions, and your demeanor or energy impact those around you. In addition, you are aware of how you interact with your environment and the effect you have on various constellations, such as your family, your team, your organization, your community, and the planet in general.

Being truly aware means that you are awake in the moment. It means that you are cognizant of the constant feedback loop in the world and the interconnectedness of all things. There is a cause and effect to everything. Every action carries with it a subsequent reaction. You need to take responsibility for yourself. Once you see how you have impacted another person, you cannot help but acknowledge responsibility for that impact. Leadership is a great privilege, and this privilege carries with it a great responsibility.

Awareness enables you to maintain sound judgment and make better decisions because moment by moment you'll see what is arising within you. You won't be blindsided or hijacked by emotions that are out of control. When you are aware of feel (the physical sensations associated with the emotions that you experience), and you remain aware of these sensations, you remain in control. The reason for this is that feel unchecked drives behavior. When you are angry that your team is not performing to your standards and you yell at them or you are cutting, derogatory, and sarcastic, there is a good chance that you are no longer in control. Typically, the sensations in your body are so great that you just blurt out what comes to mind, without listening to your internal censor. When you've said things you later regret, you may notice that you experienced strong sensations in your mouth or throat, among other parts of the body. Notice these areas next time you are about to blurt out something that would be best left unsaid or said more delicately.

You might say, "But I had every reason to be angry." The issue is not that you experienced anger; the issue is the behavior that followed. If people feel intimidated, their own feel gets activated, and then you have two people who are interacting but not listening to one another. Instead, two egos are interacting, with one on the offensive and the other on the defensive. As a leader, your main interest should be to enable your team or staff to live up to their potential. This helps you and them to be most successful.

Imagine that you are dealing with a challenging stake-holder, for example, the investment community, or those who regulate your industry. If you are not aware, you may become defensive about what this stakeholder says about your company or your leadership. In fact, before you know it, you may be arguing with the stakeholder or defending your position without truly listening.

The reality is that those who are challenging you may be mistaken or have interpreted information incorrectly. If you are truly aware of how you are responding emotionally, you are in a better position to set the record straight. This may potentially alter the action the stakeholder takes regarding your company and put you in a more favorable position. If, however, you overreact and get angry without awareness, you are likely to make your situation worse and to put yourself in a disadvantageous negotiating position. You may even be faced with having to repair an important relationship.

There is also the possibility that the stakeholder may be correct. You may not like what the stakeholder has to say, but if you are aware, you may realize that the conclusions have a grain of truth or that they are painful but sound. If you are really open, you may be able to take advantage of the lesson. This could put you in an even stronger position going forward. It also signals to others that you are willing to listen. From this place of apparent vulnerability you can generate great strength and credibility.

Leaders who are aware are coachable. They acknowledge that they don't know everything. They signal that they are willing to learn from those who are worthy of being listened to. The reality is that it's lonely at the top. Leaders have few people to confide in.

But they have a huge opportunity for being coached. They have access to talent, to knowledgeable people in different walks of life and different fields. And they don't need to be in a formal coaching relationship with those people in order to benefit from the mind–set of allowing themselves to be coached.

People who are coachable are like putty in the hands of the universe. They don't let their egos get in the way of their growth and transformation, and as a result, they put themselves and their organizations in advantageous positions. Others will often give them more information because of their openness and willingness to acknowledge that they may not have all the answers. This puts them in a good position to make decisions with more complete information.

MINDFUL MAKEOVER

The Scenario

You are conducting a one-on-one performance review with an individual who has performed well all year but who in recent weeks has made several significant mistakes.

Before

You may be so upset by the recent poor performance that you disregard the person's high performance throughout the year, focusing only on her errors and blaming her for the negative outcomes. This creates the probability that your employee will become defensive, angry, and demoralized.

Or you may focus only on the good performance and not deal with the recent performance issues. You may be uncomfortable about giving bad news or having a difficult conversation. Your stomach might be in knots, and as a result, you avoid what you might view as confrontation.

With either approach, the performance isn't appropriately appraised, and future issues will invariably arise as a result.

After

As a mindful leader, you are self-aware. You know you are disappointed in the individual's recent performance, but you are appreciative and conscious of her good performance throughout the rest of the year. You are also aware that the way in which you handle this situation will impact your employee's motivation, and you want to use every opportunity to mentor her.

As you prepare for the meeting, and during the discussion, you are aware of your thoughts, in the form of images or internal talk. But, and this is key, you are also aware of the sensations in your body (feel space). Perhaps your stomach is in knots about the difficult conversation to come. By being aware of the tightness in your stomach and accepting it, you prevent it from driving your behavior and causing you to avoid what needs to be said. You will be controlling your mind, rather than it controlling you. And you can use this opportunity to get a good employee back on track.

Internal Awareness

I want to emphasize again that this is all learnable: you can train yourself to be aware. The mindfulness technique that directly pertains to cultivating awareness is Internal Awareness, described in Chapter 3. Internal Awareness focuses on the thinking mind and the feeling body.

The Thinking Mind

The thinking mind includes the images you see on your mental screen with your eyes closed and the internal talk you have in your head. When you say you have had a thought, one of three things is happening:

- You see an image or a moving picture in your head.

- You have a conversation or tell yourself a story.

- You both see an image and talk to yourself, each of these reinforcing the other.

The Feeling Body

When you are moved to action or when you are obsessed with a thought, there is something at play here other than your thoughts. In these instances, one or more physical sensations in your body reinforce the thought. This feel is merely a physical sensation associated with emotion. For the most part, attention goes to our minds, our thoughts. We tend to think that all answers reside there. But that could not be further from the truth.

When you are caught up in emotion, what is really going on is that you may be lost in your thoughts and not realize that it's the sensations in your body that are calling the shots. Feel that goes unchecked or unnoticed will unwittingly drive your behavior. What many of us don't realize is that the body and the mind are communicating with one another all the time. If you're not trained in mindfulness, you will likely be paying attention to your mind and not notice that your body may be communicating something quite different.

When you value logic at the expense of intuition, you may not be seeing the whole picture. As you pay attention to both the thinking mind and the feeling body, you gain control and will not be hijacked by emotion. You are then able to see what is really going on and are not blinded by anger or fear, for example.

I described in Chapter 3 how this technique works when you are doing a formal meditation practice. Below I describe some mindfulness-in-action strategies that will help you to further develop awareness.

Strategies for Mindfulness in Action

This is where the rubber meets the road. Practicing the formal technique will help you to deepen your Internal Awareness. But it's the ability to be mindful as you move through your day that will really make a difference in your life, professionally and personally.

Returning to the example used earlier in the chapter, Internal Awareness is a strategy that you could use if you were challenged by a significant stakeholder. The instinctive reaction might be to get angry or impatient, to get defensive or maybe to go on the offense. But now you would be aware that this sensation is arising.

The first thing to do as you are listening to the stakeholder is to become aware of your body. If you are experiencing an emotion, you will definitely be experiencing one or more sensations in your body. If the emotion is strong enough, you may be experiencing sensations throughout your entire body. The first step in taking control is being aware of these sensations.

The second step is tracking them. They may be getting stronger or weaker, they may be spreading or deepening. What matters is that you maintain awareness. If your mind wanders, gently bring it right back to the sensations. As long as you maintain awareness of the sensations, you will be in a position to respond rather than react. Feel always drives behavior if it is unchecked. As long as you track feel, you will be in control of what you say and what you do.

The next thing you want to do is apply equanimity to these sensations. This means that you accept the fact that you are angry or fearful or whatever is arising for you as a result of being challenged by the stakeholder. Equanimity means giving yourself permission to feel. You accept the sensations arising within you, allowing them to arise in your feel space. This is a state of maintaining control; there is no acting out in these circumstances. Behavior is under control because you are responding, not reacting. As a result, you are less likely to become defensive and better able to ask for clarification and to determine what is causing the stakeholder's concern. From that place of equanimity you are better able to determine if you need to alter the organization's course of action or clarify your position and maintain course.

Now a note about equanimity. This concept involves accepting what is arising in your sensory experience. Equanimity means you accept what is. In the external world, it means that you accept that which cannot be changed. If something can be changed, by all means change it if you wish. But, of course, change it from a place of equanimity. When you are equanimous, you see things very clearly. You are not rocked by what is going on around you; rather, you act from a place of wisdom.

You can also use Internal Awareness as a strategy in action when working with your team. Let's say you assigned a key project and the team has let you down. The work is not at the level you expected or require. If you fly off the handle, you are unlikely to get the best work from them. If they didn't perform well the first time, they are unlikely to perform better if you are irate.

You have an alternative. Of course you will be angry or disappointed. But in this alternative you will be aware of what is going on internally for you. You can track the sensations so they don't drive your behavior. This does not mean that you will not express your disappointment or anger. It means that you will do so equanimously. By tracking the sensations and being equanimous with what is arising within you, you will know if you need to be gentle with the team and the guidance you need to give them, or if you need to be sharp to deliver your message. From that place of equanimity you will know what action to take, and that action will be free of your ego. Thus there will be a greater likelihood that you will get what you need and want.

When you operate from this place of awareness, it's not personal, and this gives all parties a chance to correct their action without jeopardizing relationships. When a leader intimidates his or her staff, the staff don't do their best work. The objective should always be getting the best performance possible. It is always about sustainable performance.

Practice this strategy of Internal Awareness as you move through your day. Anytime you experience any strong emotion, whether it is pleasant or unpleasant, tune in to your body and see where you are experiencing the sensation. This will get you into the habit of tuning in to yourself and will make you more familiar with your body so that, with practice and in time, you will be able to respond this way spontaneously when it matters most.

You may be thinking that it will be overwhelming to be in a difficult situation, dealing with difficult emotions, trying to listen to what is being said, and also tracking your own feel. At first it is tough. It takes practice. But the more you practice, the easier it is. You'll soon find that you are able to divide your attention effectively so that you are truly listening, and at the same time, tracking what is arising within you.

Sometimes people ask me if this will make them appear weak as a leader. The answer is an emphatic no. To the contrary, it takes great strength to be in control of your emotions and channel them wisely without denying or suppressing what you are experiencing. This is what it is to be fully aware and a mindful leader.

Chapter 8

Be Calm

We sometimes mistakenly think that some people are calm naturally and others are not, as if the ability to be calm is something you either are or aren't born with. This could not be further from the truth. Certainly, some people may appear to have a greater predisposition toward calmness. But calmness and relaxation are completely learnable and available to anyone who wishes to attain them. And a leader with the ability to be calm regardless of circumstances and who can create calm at will is invaluable.

In Chapter 2 I discussed the benefits of mindfulness and the research that highlights the physical and mental health benefits of a regular meditation practice. By meditating regularly, you alter yourself physiologically, rewiring your brain toward greater calmness and greater happiness. That is very exciting, and for those of us who like to have some measure of control, it can be very reassuring and empowering.

As a leader, you know that what you say and do is carefully scrutinized. People in your company look to you to see how things are going and how safe their jobs are. What you say and do signals to them if they have anything to worry about. And what may appear as a meaningless sign of concern, agitation, or anxiety to you may mean something quite different to your employees and other stakeholders. A leader who can remain calm under any circumstance serves to reassure others that a difficult situation is manageable and under control. This allows employees to face challenges from the perspective of problem solving rather than from a place of stress and anxiety.

And even if you are really good at hiding your stress or anxiety from others, it will never go unnoticed by your own mind and, even more importantly, by your body. The body always notices, and it never forgets. In the previous chapter I talked about how feel in the body drives behavior. The feel that is created from stress has tremendous impact on your well-being. Over time, this stress will take a toll on your mental and physical health. Stress cannot be hidden forever. Eventually, it also takes a toll on your personal and professional relationships. And if stress is not under control, it will impact your effectiveness and visible performance.

The other thing that stress does is rob you of pleasure and fulfillment, at work and at home. If you are stressed at work and are unable to decrease and manage the stress, it will also impact your personal life. You will be less likely to be present with your spouse, engaged with your children, or attuned to your pets. Remember, life happens only in the present. Miss this present moment and you miss life. In its extreme form, you will find you are not really a part of your family's life but instead simply an outsider who goes to work and comes home, never really connecting with others. This may sound extreme but is more common than you might think.

There are two aspects to dealing with stress. The first is to decrease or eliminate unnecessary stress. The second is to effectively manage unavoidable stress. Life regularly presents us with unavoidable challenges and, at times, calamity. That is what it is to live. However, much of the stress we experience in a given day is avoidable. What I mean by this is that we bring it upon ourselves, like when we pack more into an hour than is humanly possible to accomplish, when we give ourselves 15 minutes to get to a destination that is 45 minutes away, or when we double book ourselves for meetings. How can you possibly be relaxed when you are in one meeting and know that you are expected down the hall at another? Any normal human being would be tense under such circumstances.

The first step toward achieving calm is to examine your life. Honestly assess where there is avoidable stress and eliminate it. You may experience internal resistance to this. If you do, know that one or more of the hindrances are at play. You know what to do with this. Be honest with yourself and work to change your behavior. To create lasting change, you need to work with Internal Awareness (for a refresher on this technique, see Chapter 3).

Now you will be left with unavoidable stress. In Chapter 3 I describe relaxation techniques that will be helpful in managing this stress. Below I describe techniques you can use daily in your life, as well as mindfulness-in-action strategies you can use throughout the day that will help you manage stress effectively. By being deliberate about cultivating calmness in your life, you will fundamentally change the way you experience your life and the way you interact with those you lead.

The reality is that calmness and relaxation generate mental and physical power. They enable you to make better decisions because you are more able to be present and aware. Consequently, you are less likely to be impulsive and more likely to be able to widen the gap between stimulus and response. In that gap is your power—it affords you the opportunity to choose a response rather than impulsively react to the circumstances, or your mistaken interpretation of the circumstances.

In that gap you can become aware of a stillness that is always there. That is the place from which wisdom arises. Here is the source of your brilliant ideas and moments of inspiration, your great discoveries. All you need to do is listen. It is very unlikely that you will ever experience that stillness if you are stressed, anxious, or agitated. That is one of the reasons why cultivating that stillness is so important.

MINDFUL MAKEOVER

The Scenario

You are meeting with your most important prospect and you really want the account. Getting this account would make a big difference to your business.

Before

You feel tense because you want this deal so badly. You can feel your muscles are tight, and you're breathing irregularly. The stress and tension cause you to sell too hard. You go off message, waver from your plan, and give up too much to try to get the deal.

After

As a mindful leader, you are aware of how important this meeting is to your business. You feel the tension rising in your body, and you are breathing irregularly even as you prepare for the meeting. As you become aware of the tension, you take a few deep breaths to help you relax. You systematically look for the tension in your body and relax the affected muscles. Then you develop your game plan so that you are clear about your negotiating position and how far you are willing to compromise on any aspect of the deal.

At the meeting you do exactly the same thing: you are aware of your breath and any tension that might be in your body as the meeting progresses. When you feel the tension rise because you want the deal too desperately, you relax your body. This is invisible to everyone but you, yet it enables you to maintain perspective, knowing that you want the deal but that you will not give everything away to get it.

Relaxation Techniques

It is possible to systematically train yourself to develop the ability to be calm. At first you will need to actively apply the various relevant techniques, but with practice you will notice that you will be able to experience calmness and relaxation more quickly. Soon calmness will arise spontaneously, even under circumstances of personal and professional crisis.

Always think of breath as your ally. As part of your daily meditation practice, take a few minutes to tune in to your breath. Notice how you breathe. If your breaths are regular and substantial, continue breathing that way for two or three minutes before moving on to another technique. If, however, your breathing is irregular or very shallow, deepen it a bit and breathe regularly, ensuring that the in and out breaths are of even measure, say, for a count of three or four.

Another way to train yourself to be calm and relaxed is to pay attention to your body. You may wish to start and end your day by focusing on and relaxing your body. As you lie in bed, become aware of your body. Then systematically move from your toes all the way up to your head, relaxing each body part as you go: relax the feet, then the lower legs, then the thighs, moving up to the torso, the shoulders and arms, the neck, and the head. Your mind may wander many times, but by now you know what to do. Just gently come back to the body part you are working with and continue.

Over time, you will notice that you will be able to relax your body more deeply. You will also notice that you will be able to do this more quickly. Eventually, you will notice that a relaxed body (or at least a more relaxed body) will be your normal state of being.

Strategies for Mindfulness in Action

As you read above, the body and the mind are constantly communicating. Sometimes you will be conscious of what they are saying, and sometimes you will be unaware. Your mind looks to your body to see if there is a reason to be concerned. If your body is tight, your mind will interpret that there is a need to be on alert. Similarly, your body looks to your mind for clues. If your mind is agitated, your body will become tighter. This quickly becomes a vicious cycle. If the cycle is not broken, there is the possibility that you will feel anxious or even out of control.

The most effective and direct way to stop this cycle is to deliberately relax your body. No matter what is going on in your mind, work to relax your body—your mind will eventually follow suit. It's very difficult to create calmness through the mind. The body is your most effective route to relaxation and anxiety reduction. With practice you can train yourself to maintain a relaxed body throughout the day. When a relaxed body becomes your default, at the first sign of muscles tensing up you are more likely to automatically release the tense muscles. This will create the gap you need to determine if you need to eliminate avoidable stress or if you need to manage unavoidable stress more deliberately.

You can train yourself to be calm throughout the day. There is actually nothing you need to do in your day that requires a tight body. Everything you do can benefit from your body being relaxed, whether you're in a meeting, having a conversation, walking down the street, driving, swinging a golf club, or hitting a tennis ball. Have you ever noticed how much easier it is to have a conversation with someone who is relaxed? People who are agitated are more likely to detract from their message due to their visible agitation.

You can do several things during the day to train yourself to relax. For example, every time the phone rings, deliberately take a breath before you answer it. This can become your reminder to relax your body and remain relaxed during the conversation, regardless of whom you are speaking with or the topic at hand.

Every time you sit down to meet with someone, become aware of taking a breath. This is invisible to others; you are not doing anything unusual. You are merely focusing attention on your breath for a few moments. This can serve to remind you to be right here right now.

If you need to have a difficult conversation with a colleague or subordinate, notice your body. If parts of it are tight, relax them. You may notice your shoulders are tight. If so, release them and let them naturally slope. If your jaw is clenched, release it by slightly separating your teeth. This is not visible to anyone else, but it will make a huge difference for you— there will be an immediate relaxation in the mouth and jaw. You may notice that your arms are tightly folded around your body. If so, unfold them and let them rest comfortably on your lap. These simple releases will make a huge difference in your ability to create calm.

When you are walking, cycling, or driving and you are stopped by a red light, rather than be frustrated and annoyed that you are being slowed down, be grateful for the opportunity to connect to your body through your breath. Become aware of your breathing. Connect to your breath, become aware of your body, and then use the breath to melt away any tension in your body as you breathe out. It is simple and quick, and before you know it, the red light has turned green.

When you are on the golf course, standing over the ball, pay attention to your body and train it to be relaxed: loosen up anything that is tight. You will notice that you will swing more freely and make more powerful contact with the ball. As you walk to your next shot or to the next tee box, pay attention to your body and make sure it's as relaxed as it can be. Again, your body and mind are in constant communication. How you approach the ball will have everything to do with what was happening in your mind and body in the previous moment.

And when you are speaking to a friend or your family, allow your body to relax. You will find that this simple act makes you more patient and better able to enjoy their company. A tense body by its very nature makes you impatient, as if you need to prematurely move to the next thing because time is running out. Very often it's the effect of stress or an agitated mind that makes you impatient. But this impatience makes people less likely to be at ease and share things with you. Consequently, you obtain less information. You'll know less about the other person or situation and may inappropriately jump to conclusions or make decisions with limited information. It also gives the other person the impression that you are not interested in what they have to say or that they don't matter. Over time, this can damage any relationship.

By relaxing your body when you speak to another person, you will experience the patience required to deal with the silence that naturally occurs in any conversation. There is a great deal communicated in silence. To be comfortable with silence in the presence of others is a very powerful thing. In that silence you give the other person the opportunity to say things that may have been previously impossible to share. The more you practice being in that silence, the more you will become aware of a deep stillness that is always there. It's from the stillness that all wisdom and creativity arise.

Chapter 9

Be Focused

Many people think that the ability to focus or concentrate should come naturally and that when we don't focus it's because we're not trying hard enough—if only we would try harder, it would happen. This is an erroneous view and an incorrect conclusion. The untrained mind has huge difficulty in concentrating on anything for more than a few seconds, let alone a couple of minutes at a time. In Chapter 2 I shared with you the most recent research on this topic.

I also talked about multitasking in Chapter 2, which is one of the greatest impediments to the ability to focus. It is a malaise of our time and a hindrance to optimal effectiveness, sustained performance, and creativity or inspiration. If we can't concentrate on one thing, what makes us think that we will be able to concentrate on five things at a time? It defies logic. In fact, as noted in research coming out of Stanford University, multitaskers don't focus as well as non-multitaskers, are more distractible, and are weaker at shifting from one task to another and at organizing information.[1]

However, when you train your mind, you are able to concentrate on whatever you wish, for as long as you wish. This makes you highly effective and efficient. And with training and practice you can stay focused, whether under stress or in the presence of multiple opportunities or distractions. The ability to keep your eye on the ball makes all the difference between winning and losing, between utilizing and wasting resources, which can be key to successful leadership.

The ability to focus means you can be in a meeting from beginning to end without losing concentration. It means you are able to stay present when you are having a conversation or negotiating a deal. It means you can drive without your mind wandering. And it means that you can play a round of golf without thinking about the miserable shot on the last hole or the hole in one you made yesterday. It means that you can focus on what matters most to you in any given moment.

MINDFUL MAKEOVER

The Scenario

It is one of your busiest times of year. You have your annual meeting, you are finalizing your five-year strategic plan, and you are meeting with the equity analysts, all in a span of three days. You know that it will be a challenge to stay on message because of the diverse interests of various stakeholders.

Before

You know the importance of this time for you, your team, and your business. You want to be able to satisfy all stakeholders, and in so doing, you go off message. As a result, you are not consistent in your communication; you water down an important part of the message because you have lost focus by trying to appeal to all of the various interests. This is picked up by the equity analysts, and your plans are perceived to lack focus.

After

As a mindful leader, you are keenly aware of how important this time is in your business cycle and how critical it is for you to stay on message. As you meet with various stakeholders, you adjust the nuances of your message to suit the various parties, but you are consistent in everything you say and maintain a clear message, at all times staying focused and keeping your eye on the ball.

Mindfulness Training

As you know by now, you can train your mind. In fact, every technique I mention in this book trains you to focus. Every time your mind wanders and you bring it back to your object of concentration, you are developing and deepening your ability to focus. At first it seems pretty modest. Every time you start working with a technique, you wonder how long you've been doing it and how much time is left to go, you begin to think about breakfast or dinner, you are distracted by your to-do list, and so on. I always tell my clients that it doesn't matter how many times you have wandered; what matters is that you have come back. This is not intended as childish encouragement. It is absolutely true. Anyone who has trained a puppy knows that repetition matters. It doesn't matter how many times the puppy falters; you use the same positive tone and you keep at it until the puppy gets it. And in order for the puppy to get it, you really need to be patient—if you are not patient, the puppy will become agitated.

That is exactly what people need: patient, deliberate training. Getting annoyed at yourself when your mind wanders during a formal meditation is not helpful. In fact, it makes you agitated and your mind more entrenched in those thoughts to which the mind wandered. As overachievers we often will our way through things, whether it be a long work day or a marathon. But willing yourself to stay focused doesn't work one bit. In fact, if you think that you are able to will yourself to have "no thoughts," chances are you are just suppressing those thoughts, rather than not having them, and are thereby deluding yourself.

What we are after in meditation is effortless effort. Now, I know that sounds like a contradiction, but it's not. The effort you make—and here's where will is very effective—is in committing yourself to a regular meditation practice, to actually doing it. What you do when you sit for meditation is completely different. It should be effortless. Once you are sitting, you need to be as gentle as you can possibly be, noticing when you have wandered and being vigilant about gently coming back. You can be sure that this way of sitting will bring you the greatest and speediest progress.

Strategies for Mindfulness in Action

In addition to using formal meditation to increase your concentration, you can train yourself to focus during daily life, whether at the office, at home, or on the treadmill. If you intend to concentrate on anything at all and you notice that your mind has wandered, gently bring it back.

You may find yourself in a meeting that you are not leading and that, in your view, is not very useful or well run. This can cause your mind to wander as you feel aggravated or even resentful that you are wasting your time. In turn, this can cause negative reactions, such as increased blood pressure or an irresistible urge to say something inappropriate. It's also possible that you'll get lost in your own thoughts and not notice that something you disagree with has been approved. Now imagine that you have several such meetings a week, all of which trigger the same reaction. Pretty soon they'll start to take a toll on your health and well-being.

If you are being mindful, you will likely choose a different response. If you are able to get out of the meeting and spend your time in a more useful way, by all means do it. But very often it is not possible to leave such meetings. If that is the case, then see it as presenting a wonderful opportunity to practice a mindfulness-in-action strategy and to develop your ability to focus more deeply. Decide on a technique you will work with, and then stick with it. You may choose something as simple as your breath. Maintain focus on a part of your breath. If you wish to relax, choose the out breath and notice how your body relaxes every time you breathe out. When you notice that your mind has wandered, come right back to your breath.

Because you are still in the meeting, you will be dividing your attention—paying attention to what is being said in case you need to respond, and then going right back to your breath. Because you breathe all the time, this is not multitasking. You already know how to breathe and do something else. You are merely choosing an aspect of breath to work with.

You could also choose to work with sight and sound, as discussed in Chapter 6. Give what is being said and what you see your undivided attention. When you notice your mind has wandered off, very gently bring it back. Every time you come back to sight and sound you are developing your focus muscle. Think of it like reps when lifting weights.

The same strategies apply if you are at what you consider a boring function or cocktail party, say. Again, if you can choose to not participate, by all means use your time in ways you prefer. But if it's a command performance and you need to be there for your sake or someone else's, then rather than compromising your well-being or becoming exhausted from being where you don't want to be, alter your mind-set so that the situation benefits you.

This can turn a truly boring experience into a highly productive one in terms of training your mind. And, of course, anytime you increase your ability to focus or concentrate in one context, it's transferable to every other situation in your life.

Chapter 10

Be Clear

As a leader, it is essential to be clear—clear about your personal purpose, your company's vision and strategic direction, your motives and intentions, your thoughts and emotions, and your expectations for yourself and others. Essentially, when I talk about clarity, it applies to everything, both internally and in the world at large. Being clear is closely linked to being aware of what is going on within you and around you.

Being clear allows you to make better decisions. You are also more likely to be able to identify opportunities for your business and to discard proposals that are not in line with your vision. After all, a great opportunity that doesn't fit your strategy isn't a great opportunity for you. It will merely cause you to take your eye off the ball and may cause you to spread your resources, including people, time, and money, too thinly. Being clear means too that you are better able to determine who will be the most appropriate strategic partners for your business. It enables you to be proactive and to resist being driven by short-term goals or results at the expense of sustainable outcomes. When making decisions, it's important to know what is driving the decision. The clearer you are, the better you will be able to determine whether a decision is sound or based on any of the five hindrances. You will be completely aware if it is based on your purpose and strategy or on someone else's.

When you have clarity, you will know when you are distracting yourself because you don't like what you see within yourself or around you. For example, you may have experienced a situation where others in your organization assessed an individual as not performing as well as you believed that person to be doing. It's possible that the others didn't have the whole picture and didn't see what you saw. However, it's also possible that you had a blind spot. Perhaps one of your hindrances was not allowing you to see clearly. Maybe you hired the person, and your pride wouldn't let him or her fail. Only by being clear will you have a choice as to whether to make the right decision or assessment of the person's performance.

As you pay attention to clarity, you will become more easily aware when you are clear, as well as when others are clear. It will also become evident to you more quickly when you hear a presentation that lacks clarity or when a conversation seems to go around in circles. The more you look out for clarity, the more you will notice that true clarity is rare. Yet training yourself to be clear is definitely worthwhile, as you will notice how it makes you and those around you more effective and efficient. In fact, making clarity a priority signals to all those around you in the organization that it is your standard and expectation. This will prompt others to be more rigorous and disciplined in communicating with you.

MINDFUL MAKEOVER

The Scenario

You have had to update your strategy, and you need to explain the significant changes to the various stakeholders. It will be a particular challenge to explain this to employees, many of whom will be concerned that their jobs may be in jeopardy.

Before

Your inclination may be to couch things so that no one worries about losing their job. You may also be concerned that employees will feel hurt or take offense at the changes that are about to take place. As a result, your message is not clear and you water down what you intended to say. Employees hear the inconsistencies in the message and they worry that the situation is much worse than it is. The effect is that no one is clear about the vision, the strategy, or their place in the organization.

After

As a mindful leader, you are completely aware of how difficult this will be for employees. That is precisely why you pay particular attention to the clarity of your message. You ensure that the vision and strategy are clearly articulated and delivered. You know that your responsibility is to execute the new direction, and you need the support of all employees to make it happen.

(continued)

> Being clear ensures that your employees know where they stand, and they know that you are leveling with them and not sugarcoating the message. They trust what you say and can get on with making the new direction a success.

Mindfulness Training

As with focus, the ability to be clear or to develop clarity is a by-product of training your mind with the mindfulness techniques described in this book. You have an opportunity to practice being clear every time you meditate formally or use a mindfulness-in-action strategy. Being clear takes effort, so as you formally practice the techniques, be sure to be clear about what you notice. If you are working with a relaxation technique and you are relaxing different parts of the body, be clear about where the tension is; become aware of how tension in one part of the body impacts another. If you are using a relaxing breath, notice how the out breath releases tension in various parts of the body.

When working with Internal Awareness, be clear about noticing thoughts (images and internal talk) and feel sensations in the body. This technique is about dividing and conquering what is arising in the thinking mind and feeling body so that you are not overwhelmed. When you are clear about feel, image, and talk, you untangle these sensory experiences like strands. By being clear that they are really separate, you notice that they no longer have a grip on you.

The same process applies to External Awareness. When you work with sight, really see, and when you work with sound, really hear. In formal practice, clarity comes not from interpreting what you see and hear but from experiencing what you see and hear without a filter. Filtering involves judgment; instead, you want to see and hear things as they really are.

The more you practice this, the more clarity you will develop. One more tip: As you sit in formal meditation, be sure not to allow yourself to get spacey. The way you know you are spacey is that you lose or forget the technique with which you are working. For example, if you're working with Internal Awareness, you may suddenly find yourself in a relaxed state, the technique forgotten. That may seem pleasurable, but do this too long and you are not training your mind. If you notice you have spaced out, gently come back to the technique you are working with. Don't judge; know that everyone experiences spaciness at one time or another.

Strategies for Mindfulness in Action

In addition to developing your clarity through your formal practice, you will find plenty of opportunities to improve your clarity as you move through everyday life. For example, if you are in a meeting, you can choose to work with sight (what you see, such as the person who is speaking or other people in the room) and sound (the voice and tone of the person speaking). Be sure that you are hearing what is being said and not internalizing your filtered interpretation or assumption about what they must mean or intend. You might think this sounds absurd. But you would be amazed at how much we filter. Has anyone ever said to you, "I never said that," but you are sure they did? It's possible that they said what you believe they said. But be open to the possibility that you interpreted, rather than heard, what was said. And to prevent others from misinterpreting what you say, speak using mindful speech, as described in Chapter 6. By doing so, you will increasingly train yourself to say what you mean and mean what you say. As you hear yourself, you will become your own sensor for lack of clarity.

Whenever you experience lack of clarity or feel muddled or confused, it's worthwhile determining if one or more of the five hindrances are at play. The more unclear you are, the more hindrances may be getting in the way or the more powerful a hindrance may be in your life.

For example, imagine that you have received a job offer that on paper looks phenomenal. In fact, it's everything you have wanted, or so you thought—as you read the offer, you aren't so sure. The role looks very interesting, the money is what you want. Your mind says, "This is great," but your body is not at ease. Your stomach is tight, and you aren't as happy as you thought you would be. If you don't explore this situation mindfully, you will focus exclusively on the logic and you will talk yourself into the job. You might list the pros and cons to make sure the offer makes logical sense. Then you might accept the offer. And regret it later. But if you really examine what's going on, you might find that one or more hindrances are causing your lack of clarity or confusion. You may be attached to an image of yourself and what you should be doing. You may be confused about what really matters to you and not realize that you are living someone else's dream for you. Or you may be experiencing inferior pride because colleagues have been promoted above you, and taking this role would make you "equal" again. In these cases, your decision is being driven by what others value and what you have internalized, rather than by what is truly important to you.

A mindful approach to reviewing the job offer would be to examine what's going on in your body. Where are you experiencing sensations associated with being uneasy? Once you determine that, stay with the sensations so you experience the full effect. The sensations may increase greatly, they may shift, or they may spread. What will happen in this process is that clarity will follow. As you allow yourself to be quiet and experience some stillness, you will see the full effect of your body's reaction. In order to clearly hear what your body is saying, you need to listen. You need to listen without your mind censoring what your body is communicating. Once you have the complete picture, you can decide your next steps. You may choose to not accept the job because you've determined that it's not right for you. Or you may decide to accept the offer, but you will do it with your eyes wide open. You will know where the pitfalls lie and make the necessary compensations.

Another situation where you can practice clarity is on the golf course or the tennis court. When you don't feel that you are playing to your regular standard, it may be that one or more hindrances are at play. Are you playing outside yourself? Are you fixated on a particular score? Are you driven by avoiding embarrassment? If you answered affirmatively to any of these questions, the hindrances are definitely at play. And you will know this by the sensations in your body. When the body is not at ease, there is generally feel. Find the feel and stay with it. It takes practice to be able to do this as you are playing a game, but the more you practice, the better you will be at working with it in the heat of the moment. You know that when you play within yourself and you play your game, not someone else's, your performance improves and the score takes care of itself. Some days you play well and score well. Other days you play well but don't score so well. But you never perform at your best when you are not in the present moment. If you are clear in this moment, you position yourself favorably for the next moment or the next shot.

Practicing clarity provides a good opportunity to give some thought to the people with whom you spend your discretionary time. Are they truly people who energize you, who nourish you, who bring out the best in you? If the answer is yes, then you are being mindful and clear in your relationships. If, however, your relationships drain you, upset you, make you feel less than worthwhile as a human being, or you consider them to be shallow in nature, then you have an opportunity to reflect upon the reason you invest your time this way.

Time is your most valuable resource. You may find at different stages in your life that you will have more money or less money, but time is fixed. If you spend an hour doing this, you cannot spend it doing that. If some of your relationships are not positive and yet you continue to spend time with those individuals, the hindrances are likely to be at play. Examine what those hindrances might be. When you are with these people, do you experience feel sensations? What is going on that keeps you coming back? Allowing yourself to experience this fully will provide you with the answers you need to make conscious choices.

To be mindful is to be clear: to be clear about your motives, your intentions, your choices. It's not about the actual choices themselves—that is up to you. It's about choosing wisely and consciously, and knowing why you do what you do.

Chapter 11

Be Equanimous

Equanimity develops as you train your mind, just as focus and clarity do. Equanimity is not something that you have full control over. Rather, you create the groundwork for equanimity to naturally arise in your life and in your experiences.

I described equanimity in Chapter 2, and I will expand on it more fully in this chapter. From an internal point of view, equanimity refers to accepting what is arising in your sensory experience without resisting or distorting it. For example, if you are angry, allow the sensations of anger to arise in your body—don't interfere with the feel, or the physical sensations associated with your emotions.

However, at no point should you act out of the anger (or other emotion), either verbally or physically. When you are equanimous with an emotion, you locate it in the body, notice where it resides, how it may be shifting, moving, growing, weakening, or whatever it's doing. By being aware of it and tracking it, you will loosen its grip on you. The result is that you can now decide how you will behave. By being aware in this way, you are in greater control of yourself. You are in a position to respond rather than react.

From this place of equanimity you will determine exactly how you will respond. The situation may warrant that you communicate your anger or displeasure, or you may determine that this is not the time to express any anger at all. Equanimity gives you freedom; the freedom to respond in the most appropriate way, as determined by you, in any given situation. A mindful leader does not behave randomly. From a place of equanimity, the mindful leader knows exactly what is appropriate. This knowledge comes from a place of wisdom.

You may be wondering why being equanimous matters. It matters because it means you don't suffer when you experience unpleasant feel. You experience the pain that is there emotionally, but you do not suffer. The suffering is optional. It's the resistance to pain that causes suffering. As counterintuitive as it may seem, when you give the pain permission to be, it dissolves. Of course, this takes practice.

But there is also another aspect to equanimity, and this pertains to pleasant experiences. I would not want to leave you with the impression that all you can work with is pain or unpleasant experiences. When you work with that which is pleasant and you allow it to be without grasping or attaching to it, you experience fulfillment. Imagine that your company has been pursuing a large contract. The competition was stiff, and you have just found out the contract was granted to your company. Undoubtedly, you will be experiencing joy and excitement. But if your mind goes to how you hope to get more of this kind of contract and how you hope you come through and perform well, chances are that the pleasure you initially experienced will soon fizzle and may even be replaced by stress. Now, instead imagine that you have trained yourself to identify and track feel, and you know where you experience the joy and excitement in your body. As you maintain awareness of the location of these sensations, you will become aware also that the pleasure or joy is really enhanced because of your awareness of it. In fact, the more skilled you are at having a full experience of what is arising in your body, the greater the fulfillment.

Remember, when you experience equanimity internally, you can then choose your external response. This can mean that you choose to change the external situation you find yourself in. It can also mean that you choose to change nothing at all.

But how does equanimity manifest externally? What does it look like to others? What people see in an equanimous person is a deep calm and an even tone and temperament. The person is seen to be in total control, with sound decision making skills and judgment. He or she seems able to take facts into account, even in the heat of the moment, and to respond by addressing the issues rather than allowing things to get personal. Equanimous people are not derogatory, sarcastic, or insulting. Even when they call it as they see it, it is always about the situation, not the person.

There is another important aspect about an equanimous response. If someone is responding equanimously, he or she is completely comfortable saying they don't know the answer or taking responsibility when having made an error. This in itself makes that person stand out among others. Very often people feel they need to have all the answers and, rather than acknowledge an error, they are likely to blame or not take responsibility.

A final note about equanimity is that it is not an all-or-nothing state. There will be times when you are very equanimous and other times when you aren't. The reality is that it all counts. Even a small amount of equanimity will reduce suffering from an unpleasant experience or generate a good measure of fulfillment from a positive one.

MINDFUL MAKEOVER

The Scenario

Despite your best efforts and successes, the board decides to fire you as the leader of your organization.

Before

You are shocked by this and you blame certain board members, equity analysts, your team, your employees, the rating agencies, and the regulators. Your self-esteem takes a beating; you are angry, and you suffer greatly.

Because you spend so much time blaming others, you relive this very difficult situation over and over again. This deepens your suffering and does not allow you to heal. As a result, you are unable to learn from what has happened and move beyond the situation.

(continued)

After

As a mindful leader, you are aware of how difficult this is. You are initially shocked, disappointed, hurt, and angry. You allow yourself to fully experience this. You know where the feel is in your body. You are aware of the talk and image in your thoughts. And you experience it all fully with equanimity. The degree of equanimity will vary moment by moment. Some moments you will be very equanimous and other moments only moderately so. And that is perfectly fine—this is not a game of perfect. This means that you allow all of the pain to arise and, naturally, it will be significant. But by not grasping at the pain, suppressing the hurt, or denying how difficult it is, you're less likely to fall into the blaming trap. By not resisting the pain that arises, you do not experience the suffering. In time, the pain will subside and eventually dissolve.

This way of handling a difficult situation enables you to more easily get back on your feet, learn from the situation, and move on from it. The equanimity allows you to experience the pain but not the suffering. You purify any negative patterns that you experience, change what is within your control, and accept what you can't change.

Mindfulness Training

One of the most effective ways to work with equanimity is to simply allow whatever arises in your meditation to do so without pushing, pulling, denying, or suppressing it: if thoughts arise as you meditate, let them arise. If you are working with the Internal Awareness technique, then thoughts (image and talk) and feel (physical emotional sensations) are your focus of concentration. Notice them, possibly labeling them, but don't get caught up in them. Don't tell yourself stories about what is arising; just allow it to arise. Be okay with it. As you accept and allow whatever is arising, you are being equanimous. At first you will have to do this deliberately, making an effort, but with practice you will notice that much less effort will be required, and eventually the equanimity will arise spontaneously.

If you are working with External Awareness and thoughts arise, allow them to arise but make sure they remain in the background. They should not be the focus of your concentration. Instead, your focus of concentration is touch (physical sensations), sight, and sound, or a subset thereof. So when it comes to any thoughts or feel sensations in the body, do not pay attention to them or give them any energy. And it is equally important not to deny or suppress them. Think of them as background music; they're there, but you're not actively listening.

I find that there is a big misconception as to what meditation is about. Many think that it is about clearing or emptying the mind, and they become frustrated when that doesn't happen or even when thoughts arise. They believe there should be no thoughts at all, and that if there are, they have failed in their meditation or are doing something wrong. Nothing could be further from the truth. Thoughts will appear and disappear, rise and fall, for everyone. The difference between someone who is just starting to develop a mindfulness practice or who has this common misconception and someone with experience is that the experienced meditator is not disturbed by the thoughts. Instead, he or she can experience equanimity with the thoughts being there, without getting caught up in them or pushing them away. The experienced meditator allows them to arise and then automatically releases them. If you don't grasp at thoughts, they are not a problem at all. The problem lies in your relationship with thoughts. The more you apply equanimity to what is arising, the more you will create the conditions for spontaneous equanimity to become part of your life.

Strategies for Mindfulness in Action

Life offers many opportunities to practice equanimity every day. For example, when colleagues or subordinates are not approaching a situation the way you would, you may find yourself getting impatient or annoyed. This is a great opportunity to allow yourself to experience that annoyance from a place of equanimity and to see if you can just let it go or if you need to intervene. In these situations, reflect on whether it's your need for control that is causing the annoyance or would the situation, project, or client really best be served by a different approach. Leaders need to be able to judge how they can add the greatest value. By approaching any situation with equanimity, they are more likely to respond without hindrances and deal exclusively with the situation at hand.

Another example might be at performance appraisal time. Imagine you are appraising the performance of one of your key team members and you have some tough news to deliver. You know that this individual will have a very difficult time accepting any criticism, and in the past you have been reticent about dealing with the issues head-on with this individual. If you approach your feedback from a place of equanimity, you will be very aware of your own hindrances and what is arising within you. Perhaps you are tempted to avoid the conversation, but this time you choose to approach it differently. When you look for the physical sensations, you notice your stomach is tight. You maintain awareness there and you see how those sensations shift, how they get stronger and weaker as you speak. And by doing this, you remain focused on having the conversation you intended to have, rather than avoiding it.

Perhaps in your personal life a friend tells you she has just received some bad news from her doctor. Sometimes that may be hard to listen to. You are uncomfortable or distressed for the other person, but if you're honest, you're also uncomfortable for yourself. Rather than trying to take your friend's mind off the bad news so that you don't hear the pain and suffering she may be experiencing, really listen to her. Allow yourself to be completely open to that pain, no matter how excruciating it is. If you are feeling uncomfortable, you'll undoubtedly be experiencing it in your body. Locate it and stay with it. This will enable you to remain present and allow your friend to say what she needs to say. That is the greatest gift you can give to other people: to be there for them without trying to change them in any way.

Equanimity can enable you to more easily master any activity. If you are practicing the piano and do not get frustrated when you have difficulty with a particular piece, you are more likely to improve your performance. If you experience equanimity you will not become impatient with yourself and as a result are more likely to persevere, without stress and strain, until you master it.

If you are painting a canvas and the mixing of color is not to your satisfaction, equanimity will allow you to experiment without frustration or impatience. Equanimity allows you to approach what you do from a place of refining your approach rather than from a place of something being right or wrong, good or bad. This causes less stress and brings greater joy to your leisure activities.

Equanimity can even help improve your experiences on the golf course. Say you have just made the most incredible shot. You were in very thick rough, you struck the ball perfectly, and now you are putting for par. You amazed yourself and your playing partners. You're really happy. If you are not equanimous, you will put pressure on yourself, thinking about the score and the next shot you need to make, rather than being in the moment and relishing what you have just done. On the other hand, if you are equanimous, you will be aware of what is going on in your body; in this moment you will be aware of the sensations that went along with the great shot and your experience of deep pleasure. And by staying with this, you will experience fulfillment. The deeper the equanimity, the deeper the fulfillment. In fact, this will help you with the next shot. By being in the present moment, you are not carrying the baggage of stressful thinking about how you may or may not perform for the rest of the round.

When you take care of this moment, the next moment takes care of itself. Accept what is, moment by moment. If you can change a situation and wish to, by all means do so. If you can't, then be accepting of it, knowing that it is what it is. Equanimity allows you to experience peace no matter what the circumstance. It is not circumstances that create happiness; rather, your happiness is created by accepting your circumstances.

Chapter 12

Be Positive

Being positive is an integral part of being a mindful leader. Positivity is multifaceted and includes having a can-do attitude, being of service, and being grateful. It involves being a positive force in your life, your family, your organization, your community, indeed, wherever you have the opportunity to make a difference.

One of the outcomes of being positive is that you become an inspiration to those around you. You can't set out to be inspirational; you either are or you are not in any given moment. It is an outcome of your way of being. And it's a fallacy that only a select few can be inspirational. I'm not referring to charisma, which can be consciously cultivated and manipulated. I'm talking about truly inspiring others by whom and what you are, by saying what you mean and meaning what you say. You are inspiring when you capture the imaginations of those you lead, when you can communicate with passion. One of the most authentic ways of being passionate is to know your purpose in life. When you have a vision for your life and for your organization, it's easy to impart that passion. In fact, you can't help but impart it. Others will be captivated by your aspirations and your intentions. If they share the same aspirations, they will want to help you succeed. And in helping you to succeed, they become successful. You will also attract people who share your passion for what you are trying to achieve.

When you are an inspiration in this way, you help others see what they might not normally see, including their own potential. When you inspire another person, you help that person tap into his or her own greatness. When you are positive, you exude an energy that captures the imaginations of those you lead and serve, and you inspire them to aspire to achieve great things.

The activity of leadership is spontaneous. It's appropriate in the moment. It's not calculated. You trust that you will say what is appropriate in any given moment because you are present and aware of what is going on inside you and around you. You mean what you say, and you say what you mean. And you behave appropriately. You walk the talk. And you do this whether you are at work or at home with family, with friends, or in any other setting. The setting does not dictate who or what you are. There is total consistency between your professional and personal life and persona. You are a coherent, integrated being without contradiction. And this makes you comfortable in your skin. When you are comfortable, everyone notices and is more at ease with you.

Having a Can-Do Attitude

A can-do attitude is particularly helpful in solving problems or seeking opportunities. It's the attitude or frame of mind that the easy stuff we can do quickly, the impossible stuff will take more time. Leaders who are positive know that nothing that's worth doing is impossible. However, on occasion you may be presented with a really tough issue that seems insurmountable. From a strategic point of view, it's helpful to put yourself and those tasked to come up with a solution in the frame of mind that a solution exists. Your task is merely to discover it.

This discovery process starts with a very clear intention: to come up with a solution that will be beneficial to all parties involved and will do no harm. Once you have created a clear intention, your subconscious will continue to work on finding a solution, even when you aren't consciously addressing the problem. This is how great discoveries occur. There is a desire and intention to solve a problem, and there is a certainty that a solution is possible. At this point, it's most effective not to try to force a solution. In fact, the solution is most likely to naturally arise if you can still your mind. In that stillness you'll be better able to access your creativity and inspiration, and the solution will become evident. In fact, people often describe how a solution came to them while they were showering or walking down the street. In the gap between thoughts is where all solutions and great discoveries arise.

When you think there is no answer, it's sometimes helpful to ask yourself and your team this question: If what you are looking to resolve was legislated and you had no choice but to find a solution, what would you come up with? Having no out often clarifies the mind. However, it's possible that in rare circumstances there is no immediate solution. Perhaps it's because the technology necessary to solve your problem doesn't exist yet.

In that case, don't think you failed to find a solution; instead, consider that the solution is delayed by a timing issue. Or you may find that the desirable solution is financially prohibitive, so it doesn't make sense to pursue it. In such cases, you might make a business decision to postpone your move forward. But again, it's not because you couldn't adequately or positively work through the issue.

Having a can-do attitude means that you don't have a pessimistic outlook and you see possibilities in all challenges. Additionally, you choose not to tolerate pessimism in others. Pessimism is like a deadly virus. Once it infects you, you become convinced that you're doomed and, if you are influential enough, you will soon cause everyone around you to be convinced of the same non-fact.

Pessimism always carries with it one or more of the five hindrances. When someone is pessimistic, they are living in the past or the future. They are stuck in a past failure, whether perceived or real, and they project this onto what is yet to come. Or they are worried about the future and are convinced that it will not be good. Yet in the present moment there is nothing but possibility. Your responsibility as a leader is to stay in this moment so that you are a positive force for yourself and those around you.

Being of Service

Being a positive force for those around you means that you are keenly aware that your responsibility and privilege as a leader is to serve. You are here to serve your organization and the communities in which you operate, and indeed anywhere you have an opportunity to make a difference.

It takes a refined consciousness to know that the highest purpose in life is to serve. The more you formally practice meditation and apply mindfulness to your personal and professional lives, the clearer that purpose becomes. It is not something you need to force or of which you need to convince yourself. It merely arises as a certainty. Your reality becomes that you do good and you feel good. And in so doing you help countless people each day, some in small, even invisible, ways, and others in big ways. And this is all done through the activity of leadership. Being a leader is not a role but an activity. It's being a positive influence on those you have contact with every day.

But what does it mean to be of service? You are of service when you do what needs to be done in any given moment. In your organization, pitch in where you can add the most value in any given moment. This does not mean that you do someone else's job because they haven't done it. (That would be a performance issue that may require your mindful attention.) It means that you are interested in positive outcomes and you walk the talk. There is nothing more powerful than behavior. People are constantly silently—or perhaps not so silently— watching for consistency between what their leaders say and what they do.

At times, people are uncomfortable with the notion of serving because they have a misconception of what it means to serve. To serve another should never be confused with subservience. It has nothing to do with being inferior to someone else. To have the opportunity to be of service is a great privilege. We are all interconnected. Consequently, when you do something positive for another person, you also benefit yourself. There is something that awakens deep within us when we truly aspire to be of service. It brings about a sense of fulfillment.

Being Grateful

The final aspect of being positive is being grateful. There are very few birthrights. Everything we have is a blessing that can be taken away at any moment. So being grateful is merely acknowledging that you are blessed. Some days may be pretty grim. You may be experiencing misfortune or a professional or personal crisis, but even in these circumstances there is usually a blessing—the kindness of a stranger, a sunny day, a roof over your head. And on the days where there is no real crisis, you are truly fortunate. The habit of gratitude creates a mind-set and predisposition that increases the likelihood that you will attract positive things in your day and your life. You may have already noticed that your day does not seem to flow as smoothly when you are grumpy and have an ungrateful attitude. But, somehow, when you are in a state of gratitude, everything looks brighter. You don't seem to be at odds with the world, and the world is not at odds with you.

MINDFUL MAKEOVER

The Scenario

You lead a successful regional unit, which is known to be best in class. However, difficulties in other business lines within the parent company have put the entire company at risk.

Before

You are very disappointed and concerned for your own business, your job, and those of your employees. You vacillate between angrily blaming the parent company and being paralyzed by your fear. You see nothing positive in this situation, and you feel defeated and powerless. The other members of your business unit pick up on this, and they are demoralized too.

After

As a mindful leader, you know how much influence you have on the organization. You know that the entire organization looks to you for cues. You decide that the best approach is to communicate effectively with all employees. You hold town hall meetings where you are honest about the situation, and you allow a significant amount of time for answering questions and addressing concerns.

You know that you are there to serve. It is your responsibility to maintain a positive attitude while being honest and realistic.

You express your gratitude to everyone for their good work and contribution. This is not difficult to do because you are authentically grateful. Doing so significantly reduces the angst in the organization and inspires people to continue to do their best under the circumstances.

Mindfulness Training

You can train yourself to consciously be positive by using the formal technique of Imagining Positive Outcomes. Below is a snapshot of this technique; see Chapter 3 for further details.

First you need to decide what you wish to work on. It may be that you have to give an important presentation and would like to envision being able to communicate clearly, connecting well with the audience, and doing it with ease. In your mind's eye (image space), create a clear image of yourself succeeding. Visualize the room you're in and the audience. See yourself making the presentation and comfortably connecting with the participants. In formal practice it is easier to concentrate on an image with eyes closed, although some people are comfortable imaging or being aware of what they see in the mind's eye with their eyes open. In the talk space in your head, create a word or series of words that support this image of success, such as "I am clear and at ease." Repeat this to yourself at a leisurely pace over and over again. If you become distracted, come back to the image and the talk you have created.

Always imagine that the success is happening in this moment. Not that it *will* happen but that it *is* happening. As you practice this, an internal confidence will arise. Deep in your mind and body you are creating the knowledge that you can do this, that you have a measure of control over your performance and your responses.

You can apply this technique to a situation like that described above or to a specific behavior you wish to change. Whether you would like to be calmer, more patient, or less angry, the technique is the same. In image space, imagine yourself as having the behavior or characteristic you seek. Decide on a word, phrase, or sentence that supports the image, and repeat it over and over again at a leisurely pace. However, to change behavior, this technique alone will not suffice. You also need to use the technique of Internal Awareness to help you go deeply into what underlies the specific behavior. These two techniques in combination are both powerful and empowering.

If you are seeking a positive outcome for a specific situation, spend at least 10 minutes each day working on it. I consider this kind of preparation as important as working with the content of any meeting or presentation. In fact, I have made it a habit to prepare for any presentation, negotiation, or meeting by spending a few minutes ahead of time imaging a successful outcome. The aspiration you bring to any interaction is always critical. My habit is to expect the best, to seek solutions, and to create mutually beneficial outcomes. I am rarely disappointed.

Strategies for Mindfulness in Action

There are many opportunities each day to practice being positive. The first is to work with intention. You may wish to get into the habit of creating an intention for each day when you wake up. This is very simple and takes only a few moments. Imagine your day being positive, filled with opportunities to be of service, to do interesting work, to have enjoyable conversations, and so on. In addition, before an interaction you think might be challenging, take a few moments to be present and to imagine a positive outcome.

You can also practice being positive as you end your day, either before you leave the office or before you go to sleep. Take a few moments and in your mind's eye see all the things for which you are grateful. If you prefer, you can talk silently in your head and detail all the things for which you are grateful. You may be grateful for something very specific, such as a great account you won, or for something simple, like the sun shining, your enjoyment speaking with your family, or the food on your table. Often, when a client of mine feels a little flat or in a rut, I suggest practicing gratitude very deliberately in formal practice and throughout the day. Generally, the client feels transformed after only a week of diligent practice.

Another way to deliberately practice being positive is to notice how you speak to yourself throughout the day. Most of us speak to ourselves all day long. The quality of your internal conversation matters greatly. If you are in the habit of speaking positively to yourself, that's wonderful—continue doing what you are doing. But many people are not so charitable. In fact, we tend to be harder on ourselves than anyone else could be. For many people, the way they speak to themselves would be nothing short of intolerable if it came from someone else. But when it comes to ourselves, we may do this all day long, and it generally goes unnoticed.

But nothing goes unnoticed by the body. Every time you speak sharply, critically, judgmentally, meanly to yourself, your body bears the brunt of it. And it believes what you say. How could it know otherwise? This is how patterns are ingrained. A mental habit becomes a sentence, a sentence we give ourselves. We enslave our own minds. We become accustomed to being treated badly by ourselves, and then when we are treated poorly by others, we may tolerate it because we think that their judgment is justified.

Many high achievers are very self-critical. Perfectionism is also a source of self-criticism, because it's impossible to measure up. Be aware that this tendency will limit you as a leader. If you are critical of yourself, it will inevitably extend to others. It is very difficult to work for someone who is constantly critical, either verbally or by implication. A leader who does this will not draw out the best in others and will compromise his or her organization's performance.

It is critical to break the habit of negative self-talk if it plays a role in your life. Develop the habit of regularly tuning in to talk space. Notice what you are saying to yourself. Initially, this will be all you will do. For a few days just notice what you say to yourself. What proportion of what you say is critical or judgmental about yourself? The next step is to notice your body's response when you are self-critical or derogatory. You will notice that one or more parts of your body become tight and uncomfortable. This makes you even more uneasy. Since the body and mind are constantly communicating, verbal abuse in the mind is felt in the body. The final step is to set the intention that you are going to eradicate negative self-talk. Become vigilant. If you notice that you are negative with yourself, just stop. Do not allow the judgment to continue; refuse to participate in the internal conversation.

At first you may think that this strategy causes more negative talk, but I assure you this is not the case. You will become more aware of what is going on internally. Just be persistent, and you will break the habit.

Chapter 13

Be Compassionate

Compassion is rarely truly understood. It's often seen as weakness, something like a bleeding heart. And because it may be seen as a weakness, it is considered by some to have no place in leadership. But, in fact, this could not be further from the truth.

It takes great strength and courage to be compassionate. True compassion is deep caring without attachment. This is not the same as deep caring with detachment, which would imply an arm's-length relationship that does not touch you, where you could not feel the pain or get hurt in the process of caring. Rather, I am talking about caring deeply but not being attached to the outcome.

Consider for a moment how difficult that actually is. You care deeply about a person, circumstance, situation, business, or cause, but you are not attached to the outcome of your intervention or the outcome of what occurs. That is true compassion. There is real wisdom in this. And you always want the appropriate blend of wisdom and compassion. Not enough wisdom and you risk being a bleeding heart. Not enough compassion and you risk being cruel.

Let me share with you a couple of examples. You have been mentoring an individual and you care about them and very much want them to succeed. You spend time with them, helping them in particular with political issues and how to position themselves and their work. Your priority and energy goes to enabling them. But you are very aware that the outcome (their success) is not in your hands and you completely accept that with equanimity.

In another instance, you are fundraising for a particular cause that you think is worthy of your support. You do your very best to raise awareness and the funds required to launch significant initiatives. You work diligently without attachment to whether your efforts succeed or don't succeed. This is possible because you know that ultimately you do not control the end result. You can influence people but you can't force them to donate. The key in not being attached is equanimity. And this is possible because your ego is not intertwined in any success or failure. You do your best, under the circumstances, and you let the results take care of themselves.

Many people would acknowledge that if they put their efforts behind someone or something, they want him or her to succeed, or things to work out. That is perfectly normal. However, some people become desperate for it to work. And if it doesn't, they are so vested in the effort that they're tempted to blame the person, organization, government, whomever, for the failure.

In this case, were they really compassionate at all? There may have been some element of caring. But what was really in play was ego. It was about the helper, not the person who was helped. In fact, what may really matter to the helper is the end result—perhaps someone else's career was turned around because the helper gave that person a job. And there may even be one of the hindrances, superior pride, influencing all the caring the helper does or the help he or she provides.

Compassion acknowledges that everyone and everything is connected. The entire world functions as a system. Whether we are talking about systems theory in mathematics, biology, ecology, the human body, a family, or an organization, everything impacts everything else. Affect one part of the system and there is an effect in the entire system. This awareness alone should be motivation enough to help and be of service.

But there is something much deeper that happens when you express deep caring: you actually help yourself. Most people will readily admit that the process of helping someone else made them feel really good. World religions and philosophies have promoted this for centuries. And, using functional MRIs, Western science has come to the same conclusion. In fact, when individuals meditate on compassion, dramatic changes appear in their brains. Interestingly, meditation practice has long been found to significantly increase brain activity in the part of the brain responsible for positive emotions and traits like optimism and resilience—the left prefrontal cortex. Dr. Richard Davidson, a neuroscientist at the University of Wisconsin–Madison, believes that compassion can be learned and that the process can be measured scientifically: "There is increased activity not only in the prefrontal cortex, which floods [people] with well-being, but also in the areas involving motor planning.

It seems that they are not just 'feeling' good; their brains have primed their bodies to spring up and 'do' good."[1]

For a mindful leader, the ability to experience and express compassion is critical. For some people, this may be obvious and compassion may form a natural part of their personal and professional lives. To others, the thought of being compassionate may make them bristle. They fear being seen as too soft and sensitive and worry that they may be taken advantage of, that their decision making may become clouded, or that they and their organizations may become less competitive. If this is the case with you, remember that compassion is deep caring without attachment. And give some thought to the benefits that you experience physiologically when you are compassionate, and to the potential benefits for your organization. For example, when you express compassion toward another person, you clearly help them. And a little gentleness goes a long way, because it also positively impacts all those who witness it. What it communicates is that it's not "all about me," that everyone matters, that you are a team and every member of the team matters. In fact, it takes the entire team to win a game, a championship, an account, or to succeed in the marketplace. Teams that are able to function effectively together win together.

I have heard many people express concern that if they are always thinking of being compassionate toward others, they risk neglecting themselves. And this is a legitimate concern. However, keep in mind that before you can be truly compassionate toward another person, you must first be compassionate toward yourself. Think of it as putting on your own oxygen mask on an airplane before helping a fellow passenger. The only way to be compassionate and resilient without wearing down is to focus on the necessary self-compassion. From that place you can then be compassionate toward others. When you do this, you continuously replenish yourself.

To be compassionate is to contribute to creating a gentler, kinder relationship with yourself, your family, your organization, your community, and the world.

MINDFUL MAKEOVER

The Scenario

Your company has invested a great deal of time and energy in attempting to make an acquisition that would have been transformative for the company. Unfortunately, it was not successful in its bid.

Before

The fact that the company was not successful might overshadow the fact that a great deal was gained in the process. You might blame those who worked on the acquisition for not having worked hard enough or well enough, or you might blame yourself. Alternatively, you might be so disappointed yourself that you don't even consider the others involved and take into account that they too might be disappointed and exhausted by the whole process.

After

As a mindful leader, you know how much you and the company wanted this acquisition. You cared deeply, but you are not attached to the outcome. Yes, you experience disappointment, but the fact that you are not attached enables you to move on to other opportunities without lamenting or regretting the past. You acknowledge what you lost and you move on. This allows you to learn from the situation.

You are also very aware of how much effort, time, and energy has gone into this initiative, as well as how many sacrifices everyone made along the way. You know how disappointed they are. And you communicate your gratitude to everyone who worked on the initiative and let them know that their effort wasn't for naught. You indicate that a great deal was learned along the way about your company, the market, and your competitors, and this knowledge will position you positively for the next opportunity.

By exhibiting compassion toward others, you inspire them to continue to do great work. And seeing that you care deeply but are not attached allows them to let go too.

Mindfulness Training

For some people, compassion comes quite naturally. They may even be in the habit of formally and regularly sending out positive thoughts or intentions for those in need or experiencing challenging times. For others, sending out positive thoughts or intentions to others may be something they did in their distant past or not at all.

For those of you who wish to practice compassion in formal meditation, the technique, discussed below, is the same as described in Chapter 12 on page 159, but with a minor twist. The technique is also described in detail in Chapter 3 in the discussion on Imagining Positive Outcomes, page 56.

You may choose to practice this technique on a regular basis or only when you have a specific person or situation in mind. It can be your entire practice on a given day or it can be practiced for a few minutes before or after another technique. Some people enjoy this technique so much that it becomes their daily practice.

In image space, which is the mental screen in front of or behind your closed eyes (or you may think of it as your mind's eye), create an image of the person or situation for which you wish to meditate and send positive intentions. It could be an image of yourself when you are going through a difficult time. It could be an image of someone you know who is experiencing personal or professional hardship. Or it could be a situation like a natural disaster for which you are moved to meditate. When the tsunami hit Japan in March 2011, many people wanted to do a compassion meditation for Japan. So I recorded a guided meditation with this technique specifically intended for this crisis. You can visit my blog at www.argonautaconsulting.com/blog to listen to that meditation.

Now in addition to the image, create a word, phrase, or sentence that supports the image and repeat it to yourself over and over again at a leisurely pace. If you are meditating for yourself because you are experiencing anxiety, you might say "calm" or "may I be calm." For someone else, you might say "may they heal" or "may they be well." I think you get the idea.

It may happen that as you meditate you feel in your body pleasant sensations of warm regard for yourself or others. You will recognize this as pleasant feel, that is, pleasant physical sensations associated with emotion. If this happens, allow them to grow. You will notice that your mood will be impacted, and it may bring about a sense of well-being. It's equally possible that no feel whatsoever arises. That is fine as well. It's not a necessary requirement that feel arises when you do this meditation. It's also possible that instead of pleasant feel you experience unpleasant feel. This could be in the form of worry that what you are meditating for won't happen or can't happen. For instance, you may be concerned that you will not be able to calm your anxiety. If this occurs, allow the feel to arise, but in the background. Do not give it any energy.

It's important to remember that every time you sit to do a formal practice, you are developing your ability to concentrate and focus, regardless of the technique. When you let things arise in the background without suppressing or denying them, but also without getting caught up in the situation, you are developing your powers of concentration and focus.

Strategies for Mindfulness in Action

There are many ways in which you can practice compassion in your day. In fact, you may already be doing this without realizing it. Every time you are at a presentation where someone is not performing well and you root for them to improve, you have participated in an act of kindness. You have sent a positive intention. Now it may be that the person visibly benefits or not, but one thing is for sure: you will have benefited.

I like to suggest doing random and deliberate acts of kindness. Random acts of kindness include holding the door open for someone, letting someone who looks really stressed go in front of you at the checkout counter, letting someone merge into the traffic in front of you, or listening without judgment to a colleague who is visibly distraught. You perform a simple act and expect nothing in return. We would like to think that this would be common courtesy. But unfortunately, at times, courtesy is sacrificed when we are stressed or in a hurry. Those are the times that require greater mindfulness.

You may think this is really basic, and it is. Unfortunately, you may have witnessed the decline in civility that makes for a less kind and gentle world. You may also have noticed how much you appreciate it when someone does something kind for you. When an act of kindness is done, the person who received the kindness benefits. The person who performed the act of kindness also benefits—with a sense of well-being that is scientifically measurable. And research has found that those who witness the act of kindness also benefit. So, in reality, we have the potential to be of great benefit.

You can also develop your compassion with deliberate acts of kindness. As the term implies, this is when you set out to help in some way. You may decide you will send a positive intention or good wish to anyone you encounter on the street who looks stressed. You know a neighbor is ill so you offer to shop for them. You volunteer at a food bank. You donate money to a cause or organization you know to be doing good work. If this is not presently a part of your life, consider making it so; you will be amazed at how these simple strategies can positively impact your well-being. I suggest these strategies to many people I coach, and they are astounded by the benefits they experience.

Chapter 14

Be Impeccable

The final aspect of being a mindful leader is being impeccable in your words and deeds. Impeccability includes having integrity, being honest, and being courageous. It's a tall order. It implies behaving the same way when no one is watching as when you are with others.

But being impeccable should never be confused with being perfect. That would be an unrealistic impossibility. Being impeccable entails doing your best every moment of the day, every day, under any circumstances. Some days the circumstances will be such that you perform brilliantly, perhaps at your personal best. Other days you may not be as brilliant because the circumstances won't allow for it. On those days, being impeccable entails doing the very best you can under those limiting circumstances.

Being impeccable includes the appropriate use of power. Power is a responsibility and privilege that comes with leadership. Unfortunately, it is at times misused or abused. When power is misused, there are always hindrances at play, which deny you the ability to see clearly. A mindful leader knows that power is to be used with great care. Indeed, it is to be used with deep humility. Humility is critical because those over whom you have power may be vulnerable or dependent on you in one form or another. A positive or appropriate use of power will engender trust, and trust is critical between a leader and those he or she serves.

When other people trust you, there is no need to hold anything back. They implicitly know that you would not intentionally cause them harm and that you have their best interests in mind. In its purest form, what you do for each other is unconditional. And in response you both give your best. Power and trust need to go together in order for superior performance to result. Each person performs whatever activity he or she is tasked with without holding back. Each has a common vision, and that is where the attention is focused. There is nothing personal in this process. There is no ego involved.

And that's why it's so important to know your purpose and to have a vision for your life and your business. Then you can just get on with the business of carrying out your purpose and vision, with sharing your gifts with the world in whichever context you find yourself at any given moment, and you do this willingly and joyfully. By doing so, you naturally become an inspiration to others. That is what mindful leaders do: they become an inspiration to those who are touched by them in some way. And there is nothing as powerful as being impeccable.

It is also important to remember that as a leader you are a custodian, a steward of what has been entrusted to you. The world was here before you came into the picture and will be here long after you are gone. Consequently, you should aim to add value and not cause harm in the process. It is the whole notion that you leave a place, a situation, a business in better condition than you found it. And you do this impeccably, not perfectly.

Which brings me to another point: forgiveness. I can't overemphasize the importance of this. When you have done your best and you have fallen short, or when you were not as impeccable as you might have been, remember that forgiveness is critical. After all, you are human, and it takes great courage to accept responsibility for failures or misdeeds, to make the situation right (if possible), to dust yourself off, and to renew your aspiration to be a mindful leader.

Lack of forgiveness toward yourself is often caused by guilt. And guilt is nothing more that infinite self-punishment. It is the gift that keeps on giving. If it goes unchecked and you do not work with the hindrances that are causing the guilt (and lack of forgiveness), it will control and taint everything you do, and it will influence how others work with you.

This is not to say that there is not a place for remorse. Remorse is actually healthy. It acknowledges that you may have fallen short by omission or commission. It causes you to correct what can be corrected and to commit to not intentionally perpetuating the same wrongdoing in the future. There is learning in this. It has a natural beginning and end. The remorse will go on for as long as it needs—until the learning and forgiveness has occurred, but not longer than that. Then you move on.

If you forgive another person when things don't turn out positively or that person has made a mistake, it sends the message that it's okay to make an educated guess or take a calculated risk. Unless you are able to do this, creativity will dry up, and the expectation or unspoken rule will be that unless the people around you are guaranteed a win, they need not take a chance. Blaming, particularly if done publicly, has the risk of activating a hindrance in the other person. It can cause humiliation, anger, and hurt. If the person is unskilled at processing what is arising in his or her feel space, that person's performance is likely to be negatively impacted.

I want to address the notion of perfectionism before going any further because it is the malaise of so many overachievers and high performers. Unfortunately, not managing perfectionist tendencies can compromise your health and severely impact your well-being and long-term performance. It can derail your career, destroy relationships, and compromise the quality of your life. It will also compromise your ability to be a mindful leader. It's very difficult to report to or work with a perfectionist. In fact, many people will not do their best work under such circumstances. Perfectionism eventually squeezes out creativity and in its extreme form can become obsessive in nature. You lose perspective on life, and work is no longer fun.

The problem with attempting perfection is that it doesn't take into account circumstances or context, as if performance occurs in a vacuum. No one would expect athletes to perform at their personal best every time they compete. It would be a ridiculous and unrealistic goal. In fact, when an athlete achieves a personal best, it's celebrated and recognized as a real accomplishment. Yet, as leaders we sometimes expect the impossible. And that's how being impeccable can get compromised. Some days, being impeccable is easy; other days, it's a little tougher. You may not feel kindhearted or patient. You may be tempted to take shortcuts or the easy way out. You may even feel desperate. On those days, you will notice that your equanimity is compromised.

It's always prudent to be aware when you are not equanimous. When you aren't, there are generally one or more hindrances at play. You are off center and out of balance. Attachment is a likely suspect. When you want something too badly, you are attached to it—you can practically taste it. When this happens, you risk compromising your integrity, being less than honest or forthcoming, and potentially not exhibiting the courage you generally possess.

When this arises, it's useful to reflect on purification, discussed in Chapter 2. Purification refers to clearing away negative, habitual patterns. These patterns rob you of energy and take away your freedom. You are essentially held hostage by patterns or limiting factors such as fears, worries, or the desire for approval.

The first step in purification is to notice that a hindrance is at play. And you will know this because you won't be at ease. You may not be comfortable in your own skin or your body may tighten up. Over time, you will notice the cues or physical sensations before feel controls you. Awareness goes a long way in being able to purify a pattern. The next step is to apply any of the techniques that I described in Chapter 3 and discuss in the mindfulness training section below.

MINDFUL MAKEOVER

The Scenario

One of your top performers has terminated what he considers to be a small client for his business, without looking at the significant implications for the rest of the company. This client is also a significant client of other business units. You are in a leadership meeting where this needs to be addressed.

Before

Realizing the serious implications of his actions and how they will negatively impact the company as a whole, you rant and rave and tear a strip off him in the meeting. You see your behavior as justified because he was not a team player and was selfish in his actions. You intimidate him, and everyone else around the table, so that no one on your team will do this again. In the process you humiliate him in front of his peers, and he is now in a position to resent you and become defensive. In all likelihood, your behavior will be seen as an acceptable way of treating subordinates.

After

As a mindful leader, you are aware of the serious implications of this occurrence. You know you will need to do damage control with the client. You also know that you need to use this event as a coaching and development opportunity for your top performer. At the same time, the rest of the team needs to see that you are not letting him off the hook or playing favorites.

(continued)

In the meeting, you communicate that his actions were shortsighted. He and the entire team need to understand that actions that are not in the best interest of the company are unacceptable. You clearly communicate your dissatisfaction and disappointment, and you continue the conversation in private after the meeting.

In your one-on-one meeting with your top performer, you are completely honest with your feedback and displeasure. But you are never insulting, sarcastic, or derogatory. You use this as a coaching and development opportunity.

Through your words and deeds you have shown everyone that you make appropriate use of power, you are honest and courageous in your dealings with others, and you treat everyone with integrity. At the same time, your expectations are clear.

Mindfulness Training

There is no additional formal technique to help you become impeccable. Rather, all the techniques I have described previously will have a positive impact because being impeccable will naturally arise as you practice more and more. To be impeccable you need to be self-aware. This means that you need to be clear and brutally honest with yourself about how the hindrances impact your life. It's also invaluable to know your personal purpose and vision, as well as the vision for your business. (In Chapter 5 I described how to discover and articulate this clearly for yourself.)

If there are times when you become aware that you may not be impeccable, it would be worthwhile to formally practice the Internal Awareness technique. It may be that a colleague is blamed for something and you know that she is innocent. But somehow others are so adamant that in the moment you choose not to speak up, even though you feel sick to your stomach and your chest tightens up. Know that unnoticed feel, the physical sensation(s) associated with emotion, will drive behavior each and every time. This is why it is imperative to be aware when feel arises.

When faced with such a challenge, my suggestion is to practice Internal Awareness daily until you are back in control of your behavior. In so doing you will have gone a long way toward purifying negative patterns. The good news is that when you purify a pattern in one situation it carries forward to every other situation. There is great effectiveness and efficiency in this. It's like lifting weights. The greater your stamina or strength in lifting weights, the easier it is to do things in your life that require physical endurance and strength. The benefit extends outside the gym to your entire life. The same applies to the purification of negative patterns.

Strategies for Mindfulness in Action

Opportunity to be impeccable abounds each and every day, and there may be times when we could be more impeccable. Here are a few examples:

- You know that you have no chance of meeting a launch deadline, but you withhold that information.

- You hire someone who is not well suited for the job because you are doing someone a favor.

- You bully someone into supporting you in a meeting.

- You manipulate the facts to suit your purposes.

- You use company property for your personal benefit.

- You are not as accurate as you should be on an expense claim.

- You blame others when they have made an honest error.

In each of these situations hindrances are involved. The key is to identify the hindrance that has brought you to that place. Once you have, reflect on whether this is a pattern in your life. Next, become aware of your body; notice where you might be experiencing physical sensations associated with emotion. In order to purify you must locate the sensations in your body and stay with them. Follow the sensations if they move. Do not judge yourself. Your interest is to see how these sensations are driving your behavior. As you stay with awareness, you will notice that eventually the sensations dissolve. As they do, their grip also dissolves.

You may also notice that there is internal chatter going on. You may be judging or criticizing, you may be blaming someone else, or you may be justifying your behavior. You may also be recalling images of the situation. With practice you will be able to notice what is going on in your body, as well as your thinking process—that is, your internal talk and any images.

Remember that when you work with feel, image, and talk, the idea is to notice what is arising but not to get caught up in it. If you notice that you are fueling any of it, such as continuing the internal conversation, stop immediately. Your job is to be aware of what is arising with equanimity. Allow whatever arises to do so, and then allow it to release. Do not get in the way. Otherwise you continue to fuel the drama, and it will grow. It is like a battery. If you allow it to run continuously, it will eventually die. If you keep charging it, it will go on and on. For example, when you allow feel to arise and to release, the pattern's grip on you decreases and eventually dies down. If you keep charging the battery or fueling feel, it will strengthen and control you.

It was unchecked feel that made the less than impeccable behavior possible. And you must take responsibility for this. Only you can work with your feel to purify your negative patterns. How the patterns arose in the first place is not as relevant as being aware that a hindrance is at play, locating feel, and dissolving it.

Everyone has negative patterns. They are a normal part of being human. They accumulate over a lifetime. A mindful leader can consciously and proactively clear these patterns and positively transform.

Chapter 15

Nine Ways Forward

As you have seen in the preceding chapters, each day presents countless opportunities to be a leader. These don't depend on your position in an organization, your social or economic status, or your age. Remember, leadership isn't a role, it's an activity—a leader is anyone who is in a position to influence another human being. Imagine how many times a day you are in that position, personally and professionally. What you do with those opportunities is in your hands. Mindfulness can help you make the most of them.

Mindfulness is a skill. Like all skills, it's learnable. It takes motivation, good techniques, and practice, practice, practice. As any athlete or musician knows, practice and perseverance are what distinguishes good performers from great performers. And the same applies to developing mindfulness. In fact, the more you practice, the more it will become part of who you are. You will be able to call upon every aspect of the skill at will. And increasingly you will notice that you will not even need to call upon it; it will arise naturally when circumstances require it.

Whatever you are called upon to do or whatever opportunity presents itself, you have the opportunity to be a mindful leader. It may be that you are in a formal leadership position.

However, no matter where you are in an organization, whether you are the most senior or junior person there, the same nine ways of being a mindful leader apply. In fact, companies that populate themselves with mindful leaders throughout the organization maximize their potential, create value, and have the greatest impact in the marketplace.

But before you can effectively lead another person, you need to develop self-leadership. Mindfulness training provides you with what it takes to know yourself at a very deep level. You need to know who and what you are and your purpose in life. What are you here to do? What brings you passion? What are your gifts? Without knowing your purpose and vision for your life it's difficult to lead effectively. You also need to know your negative patterns or hindrances. Hindrances hold you back from being the best you can be and from experiencing fulfillment in life. Mindfulness allows you to become aware of these hindrances and to dissolve them. Because mindful leaders are clear about their own purpose, they know the importance of defining, articulating, and communicating their organization's vision and strategy. And by doing so they are more easily able to capture the imagination and enthusiasm of their teams and the entire organization.

Their self-awareness also means mindful leaders will behave in exactly the same way whether in the boardroom, with family, on the golf course, or at the supermarket, and whether someone is watching or not. The reason is simple. No matter where they are, they are aware of the potential impact they might have and they will not waste an opportunity to serve. They intuitively know that there is no difference among us, that we are all interconnected, and that by serving others they benefit themselves.

They are well aware that the way in which they relate to their teams and employees impacts everything, from how their customers are served to innovations in product development and service delivery to their branding and market perception. All stakeholders are positively impacted. They also know that their sphere of influence goes far beyond the organization. Everyone who comes in contact with a mindful leader is impacted positively. In turn, the way those people relate to their families when they go home at night is qualitatively different. But it doesn't stop there.

Mindfulness is contagious. A mindful leader will encourage mindfulness in others. In fact, when teams are trained together, it accelerates the development of a mindful culture. Mindful people attract other mindful people to their sphere of influence. A greater proportion of clients and stakeholders are more likely to be mindful themselves or to be attracted to that way of operating. And this way of being extends to the communities the organization serves.

Mindful leaders view leadership as a responsibility and a privilege. They're at ease in their own skin and do what they have a passion for. They can't help but to enjoy their days, have fun, and experience joy. When entire teams and organizations experience their organizational lives in this way, vibrancy and creativity flow among the members of the organization, and this impacts all stakeholders and the communities in which these organizations operate.

Extensive research shows that mindfulness training positively impacts the health of those who practice it. Not only does it make them healthier, it makes them more effective and efficient, better able to make decisions, more creative, happier, and less likely to be absent from work. Health and disability costs are among the highest expenses for any organization, and organizations that have introduced meditation programs have reaped benefits to their bottom line.[1]

Mindful leaders know that the combination of being present, aware, calm, focused, clear, equanimous, positive, compassionate, and impeccable makes them better leaders, and they continuously strive to further develop these skills. Indeed, these nine ways make up your true nature, which may have been obscured by negative patterns and busyness. Busyness drives away the stillness from which all inspiration arises. Mindfulness enables you to access that stillness once again. Becoming a mindful leader is clearly a high standard. But as challenging as it may seem, it is completely learnable and achievable by everyone who aspires to it. It eventually becomes your way of being; your life is positively transformed over time, and so is everyone around you. In fact, as you move through the world as a mindful leader, you will touch the lives of many, some in big ways, some in small ways. And there will be countless people whose lives you will positively touch without even knowing it. This is what it is to live life with purpose and to be of service. By expanding the number of mindful leaders and creating a more mindful society, we can transform our lives, our organizations, and the world.

Endnotes

CHAPTER 2

[1] Shinzen Young. "Why Practice Mindfulness?" 2006. www.shinzen.org.

[2] Marc Kaufman, "Meditation Gives Brain a Charge, Study Finds," *Washington Post*, January 3, 2005.

[3] Quoted in ibid.

[4] On the six senses see Shinzen Young, "Purpose and Method of Vipassana Meditation." 2007. www.shinzen.org.

[5] Ibid.

[6] Ibid.

[7] Ruth Pennebaker, "The Mediocre Multitasker," *New York Times*, August 30, 2009; Associated Press, "Multitaskers Make Lousy Multitaskers: Study." August 24, 2009.

[8] Herbert Benson, *The Relaxation Response* (New York: Avon Books, 1975).

[9] Viktor Frankl, *Man's Search for Meaning* (New York: Beacon Press 1959 and Simon & Schuster Inc. 1984).

[10] Michelle Conlin, "Meditation: New Research Shows that it Changes the Brain in Ways that Alleviate Stress," *Business Week*, August 30, 2004.

[11] University of Sydney, "Meditation Back to Basics," *University of Sydney News*, June 10, 2011.

[12] Ibid.

13   Shinzen Young, "What Is Mindfulness?" 2007. www.shinzen.org.

14   Christopher R.K. MacLean, et al., "Effects of the Transcendental
     Meditation Program on Adaptive Mechanisms: Changes in Hormone
     Levels and Responses to Stress after 4 Months of Practice," *American
     Journal of Cardiology* (November 1996).

15   Quoted in Andrew W. Saul, "Prescription for a Happy Heart," *Vitality*,
     February 2006.

16   Jo Marchant, "How Meditation May Ward Off the Effects of Aging,"
     London Observer, April 24, 2011.

17   "In Pain, Try Meditation," *Huffington Post*, April 10, 2011.

18   Sharon Begley, *Train Your Mind, Change Your Brain* (New York: Ballantine
     Books, 2007).

19   University of Sydney, "Meditation Back to Basics," *University of Sydney
     News*, June 10, 2011.

20   Corey Criswell and André Martin, "10 Trends—A Study of Senior
     Executives' Views on the Future" (Center for Creative Leadership
     Research White Paper, Colorado Springs, 2007).

21   Elizabeth Weise, "Meditation Makes People More Rational Decision-
     Makers," *USA Today*, April 20, 2011.

22   Chris Mooney, "The Science of Why We Don't Believe Science,"
     Mother Jones, May/June 2011.

23   Conlin, "Meditation: New Research Shows that it Changes the Brain
     in Ways that Alleviate Stress."

24   Sharon Begley, "Can You Build a Better Brain?" *Newsweek*, January 3, 2011.

25   Carl Zimmer, "The Brain: Stop Paying Attention: Zoning Out Is a
     Crucial Mental State," *Discover*, June 15, 2009.

26   Roni Caryn Rabin, "Regimens: Noise Canceling, Without
     Headphones," *New York Times*, May 2, 2011.

27 Barry Boyce, "Two Sciences of Mind: Cutting-Edge Science Encounters Buddhism's 2,500-Year Study of the Mind," *Shambhala Sun*, September 2005.

28 Charles N. Alexander, et al., "Effects of the Transcendental Meditation Program on Stress Reduction, Health, and Employee Development: A Prospective Study in Two Occupational Settings," *Anxiety, Stress and Coping International* 6 (1993), 245–62.

29 Quoted in Conlin, "Meditation: New Research Shows that it Changes the Brain in Ways that Alleviate Stress."

30 Maria Gonzalez, "Organizational Health: A Strategic Imperative for Sustainable Performance" (Graduate lecture given at the Organizational Health Conference, McGill University, November 4, 2005).

31 Quoted in Virginia Galt, "Out of the Shadows: Mental Health at Work," *Globe and Mail*, March 29, 2006.

CHAPTER 3

1 Shinzen Young, "Purpose and Method of Vipassana Meditation," 2007, www.shinzen.org.

2 Shinzen Young, "The Science of Enlightenment, Teachings and Meditations for Awakening Through Self-Investigation" Sounds True Audio Learning Course, Boulder, Colorado, 1997.

3 Quoted in Steve Lohr, "Slow Down, Brave Multitasker, and Don't Read This in Traffic," *New York Times*, March 25, 2007.

4 CBC News, "Texting Increases Crash Risk 23-Fold: Study," July 28, 2009, www.cbc.ca/news.

CHAPTER 5

1 Napoleon Hill, *Think and Grow Rich* (New York: Ballantine Books, 1960).

CHAPTER 9

[1] Ruth Pennebaker, "The Mediocre Multitasker," *New York Times*, August 30, 2009; Associated Press, "Multitaskers Make Lousy Multitaskers: Study." August 24, 2009.

CHAPTER 13

[1] Penelope Green, "This Is Your Brain on Happiness," *O, the Oprah Magazine*, March 2008.

CHAPTER 15

[1] Jane Stevens, "Meditating on the Bottom Line," *Washington Post*, October 1, 1996.

Bibliography

Alexander, Charles N., et al. "Effects of the Transcendental Meditation Program on Stress Reduction, Health, and Employee Development: A Prospective Study in Two Occupational Settings." *Anxiety, Stress and Coping International* 6 (1993): 245–62.

Begley, Sharon. *Train Your Mind, Change Your Brain*. New York: Ballantine Books, 2007.

Benson, Herbert. *The Relaxation Response*. New York: Avon Books, 1975.

Boyce, Barry. "Two Sciences of Mind: Cutting-Edge Science Encounters Buddhism's 2,500-Year Study of the Mind." *Shambhala Sun*, September 2005, 34-43, 93-94, 96.

CBC News. "Texting Increases Crash Risk 23-Fold: Study." *CBC News*, July 28, 2009. www.cbc.ca/news.

Conlin, Michelle. "Meditation: New Research Shows that It Changes the Brain in Ways that Alleviate Stress." *Business Week*, August 30, 2004.

Criswell, Corey, and André Martin. "10 Trends—A Study of Senior Executives' Views on the Future." Center for Creative Leadership Research White Paper, Colorado Springs, 2007.

Frankl, Viktor. *Man's Search for Meaning*. New York: Beacon Press, 1959 and Simon & Schuster Inc., 1984.

Galt, Virginia. "Out of the Shadows: Mental Health at Work." *Globe and Mail*, March 29, 2006.

Geithner, Timothy F., and Lawrence Summers. "A New Financial Foundation." *Washington Post*, June 15, 2009.

Gonzalez, Maria. "Organizational Health: A Strategic Imperative for Sustainable Performance." Graduate lecture given at the Organizational Health Conference, McGill University, November 4, 2005.

Hill, Napoleon. *Think and Grow Rich*. New York: Ballantine Books, 1960.

Kaufman, Marc. "Meditation Gives Brain a Charge, Study Finds." *Washington Post*, January 3, 2005.

Lohr, Steve. "Slow Down, Brave Multitasker, and Don't Read This in Traffic." *New York Times*, March 25, 2007.

MacLean, Christopher R.K., et al. "Effects of the Transcendental Meditation Program on Adaptive Mechanisms: Changes in Hormone Levels and Responses to Stress after 4 Months of Practice." *American Journal of Cardiology* (November 1996).

Obama, Barack, transcript of interview with the *Wall Street Journal*, *Washington Wire*, June 16, 2009. blogs.wsj.com/washwire/2009/06/16/transcript-of-obamas-interview-with-the-journal.

Pennebaker, Ruth. "The Mediocre Multitasker." *New York Times*, August 30, 2009.

Saul, Andrew W. "Prescription for a Happy Heart." *Vitality*, February 2006.

Young, Shinzen. "Purpose and Method of Vipassana Meditation." 2007. www.shinzen.org.

———. "The Science of Enlightenment, Teachings and Meditations for Awakening through Self-Investigation." Sounds True Audio Learning Course, Boulder, Colorado, 1997.

———. "What Is Mindfulness?" 2007. www.shinzen.org.

———. "Why Practice Mindfulness?" 2006. www.shinzen.org.

Index

Maria Gonzalez, BCom, MBA

Maria is a 30-year business veteran who believes that mindfulness transforms lives and organizations, and that it has the potential to transform society. She has been meditating regularly since 1991 and teaching mindfulness since 2002. She applies mindfulness to all aspects of her life, both personally and professionally. As founder and president of Argonauta Strategic Alliances Consulting Inc., she ensures that mindfulness is indistinguishable from her business, whether negotiating complex strategic alliances, doing strategy consulting, or coaching business leaders, professionals, entire teams, or organizations in mindful leadership.

Maria has taught strategy and organization development at McGill University's Desautels Faculty of Management. Over the last two decades she has served on numerous boards and has been a member of the Corporate Advisory Board for the Harvard Medical School—MacArthur Foundation's study on depression and workplace performance. Having served as a founding member and vice-chair of the Global Business and Economic Roundtable on Addictions and Mental Health, she knows the toll stress can take on individuals, organizations, and society.

Maria has witnessed how Mindfulness meditation can positively impact personal and professional lives. Those who practice the techniques regularly benefit from reduced stress and an ability to create calm and focus at will, which enables them to make better decisions and attain greater fulfillment in their lives. Maria's personal vision is to enable and empower others to reach their full potential by helping them discover the wisdom within.

Her passion is the application of mindfulness to daily life, and she has coached hundreds of business leaders and professionals who now apply it while in meetings, making presentations, developing corporate strategies, negotiating deals, sitting on airplanes, running on treadmills, or teeing up on golf courses. Maria believes that creating mindful leaders transforms lives and organizations.

Mindful Leadership is Maria's second book. She is the coauthor of the award-winning *The Mindful Investor* (John Wiley & Sons Canada, Ltd.). You can visit her online at www.argonautaconsulting.com and read her blog at www.argonautaconsulting.com/blog.